D0948167

A Treasury of Russian Verse

A Treasury of

RUSSIAN
VERSE

Edited by

AVRAHM YARMOLINSKY

Granger Index Reprint Series

BOOKS FOR LIBRARIES PRESS
FREEPORT, NEW YORK

Copyright, 1949, by The Macmillan Company
Reprinted 1969 by arrangement with
Random House, Inc.

STANDARD BOOK NUMBER:
8369-6093-9

LIBRARY OF CONGRESS CATALOG CARD NUMBER:
79-80370

MANUFACTURED
BY
HALLMARK LITHOGRAPHERS, INC.
IN THE U.S.A.

Acknowledgments

THE EDITOR herewith thanks:

Max Eastman for permission to reprint his translation of "Message to Siberia" by Pushkin.

Robert Hillyer for permission to reprint his translation of "The Poet's Death" by Lermontov from *Centennial Essays for Pushkin*, edited by Samuel H. Cross and Ernest J. Simmons, Cambridge, Mass., copyright 1937, by the President and Fellows of Harvard College.

Frances Cornford and Esther Polianowsky Salaman for permission to reprint their translations of "I Come Again" by Foeth, "The Hay Harvest" by Maikov, "I Planted My Bright Paradise" and "The Hawk" by Blok from *Poems from the Russian*, chosen and translated by Frances Cornford and Esther Polianowsky Salaman, Faber and Faber Ltd., London, first published in 1943, all rights reserved.

Random House, Inc., New York, for permission to reprint the following poems from *The Works of Alexander Pushkin*, selected and edited with an introduction by Avrahm Yarmolinsky, copyright 1936, by Random House: "Though Soporific Not a Little," "Winter Evening," "Elegy," "On the Translation of the Iliad," "No, Never Think," "In Vain I Seek to Flee," "When Lost in Thought," "Tatyana's Letter to Onegin," "To Chaadayev," "To N. N.," "Gay Feast," "Grapes," "On Count M. S. Vorontzov," "Beneath Her Native Skies," "Arion," "The Man I Was," "Portrait," "Lovely Youth," "I Loved You Once," "Here's Winter," "Along the Noisy Streets," "My Critic," "Abandoning an Alien Country," "When in My Arms," "I Visited Again," "The Eremites of Old," "Unto Myself I Reared a Monument," "Secular Power," " 'Tis Time," "The Tale of the Golden Cockerel." Except for the first eight pieces, the translations have been revised.

Some of the poems were first published in *The New Republic*,

Poetry, The Slavonic Review (London), *Survey Graphic, Tiger's Eye,* and in the anthologies: *New Directions* 1941, *Translation* (London) 1947, *World Literature,* ed. by Christy and Wells, 1947, *People in Literature,* ed. by Loban, Cook and Stauffer, 1948, *The Heritage of European Literature,* ed. by Weatherly, Wagener, Zeydel and Yarmolinsky, 1948-9.

Foreword

THIS ANTHOLOGY covers the period from the early years of the past century down to our own day, verse written since the Revolution occupying approximately one third of the book. It contains one of Pushkin's folk tales, the entire text of *The Twelve* by Alexander Blok, a few other long poems, and some pieces, complete in themselves, taken from sequences too long to present in full. Aside from these, the volume is made up of short lyrics. The inclusions were chosen for their intrinsic merit, but a certain amount of space was allotted to verse that is primarily of documentary interest. The arrangement is roughly chronological, and as far as possible poets belonging to the same school have been placed together. In Russia writers tend to travel in groups, but it should not be forgotten that significance is a matter of distinctive individuality rather than of affiliation. The effort was to offer work representative of the period and of the poet. Limitations of space and the difficulties with which translation bristles sometimes blocked the way. Strict faithfulness to the form of the originals was not always feasible or even desirable, since the prosodic practices and resources of the two languages, while similar, are by no means identical. Nevertheless, in some instances it was possible to adhere to the meter and rhyme scheme of the original. The inexact rhyme so widely used in Russian poetry, and not unknown in English verse, was employed in several lyrics, notably those by Pasternak. The translator's first duty was held to be to the spirit of the Russian poem.

Most of the poems were done into English verse by Babette Deutsch. In the case of the few pieces done by other hands, the names of the translators are given in the table of contents.

Less than a third of the poems that make up this volume appeared in an anthology of Russian verse chosen and Englished by Babette

Deutsch and the present editor, a book first published in 1921 and subsequently revised and augmented. No more than a score of these are presented here unchanged. The rest have been revised or are given in an entirely new version.

An introductory essay offers an historical sketch of Russian poetry, and the editor has supplied footnotes where they seemed essential. There is also a biographical note on each of the poets represented. The year under the poem indicates the date of first publication, unless bracketed, when it refers to the date of composition. In a few cases, where there is a wide gap between the two dates, both are given.

A. Y.

Contents

xiv

xvi

Introduction

AS FAR AS the outside world is concerned, Russian literature may be said to have arisen when the nineteenth century was well under way. Indeed, in Russia the unbroken tradition of secular writing of the imaginative kind is not much older than two hundred years, which makes Russia's the youngest of the major literatures of the world. The Russians, like others, lisped in numbers. They developed the medium of verse before that of prose, although the latter was eventually to become their chief artistic glory. The decades between the reigns of Emperors Peter and Paul were for them a period of apprenticeship, in literature, as in other skills. The writers imitated the Greek and Roman classics, often at second-hand, and French neoclassicist poetry. Early in the nineteenth century Russia already possessed a considerable body of verse based on a prosody that later generations were merely to refine upon, and couched in a language brought close to the living speech of the cultivated public, yet using some of the resources of the stately archaic tongue of the Church books.

This verse, being largely derivative and clumsy, is of historical interest only. Gavriil Derzhavin's work is one of several exceptions. The great Catherine's courtier was a genuine, if intermittent, poet. He possessed great verve and a keen eye for movement and color, to judge by some of his descriptions, be it of a waterfall or a festive board. He dealt with the commonplaces of poetry, such as nature, God, death, in personal, if stiff, accents. The prolix poems in which, tempering flattery with irony, he celebrated the virtues of his queen or the triumphs of her armies, or again attacked injustice in high places, contain passages of unusual effectiveness. The old Sybarite's anacreontic pieces occasionally achieve a homely charm, especially when he eschews didacticism, the blight of the age. That verse with a moral can be delightful is proven by the shrewd and racy fables of Ivan Krylov (1768–1844), the Russian La Fontaine.

1

Derzhavin lived to witness Alexander's victory over Napoleon. The venerable poet bequeathed his "antique lyre," as he put it, to Vasily Zhukovsky. This young man, who had been delighting the public with ballads and patriotic poems, belonged to a generation brought up on the classics, but his work, like that of a few of his contemporaries, steered clear of solemnity, grandiloquence, heroics. Instead it stressed sentiment, revery, the claims of the heart. The new trend was short-lived and rather sterile. There was little in the Russian temperament or the Russian scene to favor this variety of early romanticism, tender-minded, dreamy-eyed, pietistic, conformist. In any event, Zhukovsky was less a poet in his own right than a translator of verse, ancient and modern, Western and Oriental. As such, he performed a signal service to the culture of his country. Literarily speaking, Russia was until recently a debtor nation, and it is a notable fact that practically every poet applied himself to making foreign verse accessible to his compatriots. Whatever defects Russian poetry may have, they have not been caused by inbreeding.

It was not Zhukovsky who presided over his country's literature as it emerged from the awkward age, but a younger and more greatly gifted writer, Alexander Pushkin. His adolescence coincided with the second decade of the new century. Those were stirring years. The victory of 1812 enhanced the national self-consciousness, fresh winds were blowing from widened horizons, liberal influences were in the air. The time was ripe for the rise of a literature rooted in the native soil yet profiting by what had been learned from the West. Pushkin was foremost in shaping this literature. His work for the first time gave it a more than local significance and allowed it to transcend the national boundaries.

There were several facets to Pushkin's genius, but he was above all a poet, the finest that has graced the language. He never lost the taste for classic sobriety and for what he called "the charm of naked simplicity" which he had acquired in his youth and which made Mérimée declare him "an Athenian captive among Scythians." The Byronic unrest that informed the verse of his early manhood was merely a passing phase. Although he loved freedom and hated bigotry and oppression, he was not a rebel. The writings of his

2

maturity had an objective, realistic quality implying an acceptance of life on its own terms. His passionate nature knew the discipline of a clear intelligence, a capacity for detachment, and a sense of measure. The foreigner, who must depend on translation, may agree with Flaubert that the Russian master, with his sanity and balance, is "flat." To the native, sensible not only of Pushkin's fine humanity, but of the unobtrusive perfection of his style, his writings are a source of pure joy. The Revolution, which has caused so many re-valuations, has only enhanced his reputation as the fountain head of his country's literature. Ranked by his compatriots with Dante, Shakespeare, Goethe, he is an object and to some degree a victim of mountainous exegesis and of a veneration that verges on a semi-official cult.

Pushkin was companioned by a group of lyricists whose work, though of a minor order, is distinguished by technical proficiency. Their verse bears the imprint of classicism but wants the tone of self-assured serenity it had in the age of Derzhavin, and some of these poets tend to the romantic. One of them, Koltzov, was a genuine folk poet. A generally serious and reflective mood prevails, though there is no lack of light and epigrammatic pieces. In some of the poems the nationalist motif is wedded to a conservative attitude; elsewhere, notably in the rather clumsy performance of the Decembrist Ryleyev, it goes hand in hand with a radical orientation. One of these poets died and another became insane before they fulfilled their rich promise. Of them all, the somber Boratynsky, whose often acidulous verse is marked by an obtruding intellection, is now best remembered.

Tyutchev, too, was a contemporary of Pushkin's, surviving him, however, by many years. Of the men who, aside from the master, made the first four decades of the nineteenth century an age of poetry, Tyutchev is perhaps the most likely to find a way to the sympathetic understanding of foreigners. His lyrical gift and fine craftsmanship were at the service of a metaphysical temperament alien to classical rationalism, explicitness, and serenity. The world of our common activities was for him a mere screen for "the ancient chaos," which is ready to engulf man, his petty works, and his

3

yearning spirit. Tyutchev did not seek to flee from this black abyss or to conceal it. Rather did he live in constant awareness of it.

The mantle of Pushkin fell not upon Tyutchev, who wrote for posterity, but upon Lermontov. This brilliant, egotistical youth was a lyricist of rare gifts. His verse follows patterns different from Pushkin's, but the effect of music and magic is as strong. His poetry is of an essentially romantic cast, expressive of a longing for the unattainable and ineffable. The growing civic bias of the mid-century made it possible to put a social interpretation on the disquietude that pervades his work and that sometimes breaks out in vitriolic satire, although he revolted less against the czar of all the Russias than against the God of heaven and earth. His imagination was haunted by the somber figure of a rebel angel vainly seeking regeneration through the love of a maiden. He had, however, moods of serenity and piety, and his verse, as indeed the work of other Russian romantics, could be sober and earthy. A realistic strain runs deep in the grain of the Russian temperament.

As he was approaching maturity, Lermontov, like Pushkin, tried his hand at prose, producing a remarkable novel, *The Hero of Our Time*. This was published in 1840. On a May morning two years later, Gogol's *Dead Souls* appeared in the bookshops. The day of prose had dawned. The period, one of the most fruitful in literary history, lasted about half a century, coinciding with the better part of the Victorian age. In the course of it, fiction held the center of the stage, the taste for poetry undergoing progressive deterioration. There was one poet, however, who rivaled in popularity, if not in importance, the contemporary novelists Turgenev, Dostoevsky, Tolstoy. This was Nekrasov. He made articulate the consciousness— and the conscience—of the period of reform and inchoate revolt which had set in with the death of Nicholas I. His was, he said truly, "the muse of grief and vengeance." His troubled, uneven verse dwelt upon the miseries of the oppressed masses and voiced the peccavi of the gentry, aware of their debt to the people, as well as the aspirations of the democratic intelligentsia. Nekrasov did not hesitate to throw untransmuted into his poems the raw stuff of satire and *feuilleton*, of parody and pamphlet. At its best, his verse conveys passionate self-scorn and stinging pity with extraordinary effectiveness. Possessed of a fine ear and deriving some of his rhythmic patterns from folksongs, he made a number of prosodic innovations.

Nekrasov set the fashion for the middle decades of the century. A socially indifferent poetry became anathema. In radical circles the utilitarian view of literature as a vehicle for enlightenment and moral uplift prevailed, and versemaking was rather looked down upon. In the serious sixties an iconoclastic "Nihilist" critic advocated the abolition of all art and laid impious hands on the laurels of Pushkin himself. In this unfriendly atmosphere several authors continued to carry on the tradition of pure poetry. Maikov studied painting in his youth, and his poems show a marked sense of line and color. He was a careful craftsman and achieved a small excellence in his genre pictures of the native scene and in his imitations of the ancients, though his was a pastiche paganism. Alexey Tolstoy had among his various gifts a talent for neat and graceful lyrics. Foeth's work was furthest removed from the concept of utilitarian art. His poems have the gossamer, insubstantial quality of revery. It has been said of this etherealist that he could have paraphrased the familiar dictum thus: I dream, therefore I am. So absorbed is he in the mood of the moment, that time abdicates for him. Indeed, some of his most successful pieces are verbless. He does not state, but adumbrates, suggests. He employs a delicate imagery in an effort to reach out toward the supersensuous and to present nature as the cosmic context of human life.

These poets professed allegiance to the principle of art for art's sake. The same attitude of aloofness from the evils of the day was shared by Karolina Pavlova, one of the first Russian bluestockings. Nevertheless, with the exception of Foeth, they all wrote political verse, as did also Tyutchev, preaching a pietistic and reactionary variety of nationalism. Polonsky alone was a middle-of-the-road liberal. It is not surprising to find that his work, which is rather mediocre, holds the middle ground between the performance of the civic-minded realists and the aloof aesthetes. Both schools of poetry reached their nadir during the eighties and the better part of the nineties, and so did the taste of the public. Those were years of bloodless, pretty, slovenly verse, plaints and platitudes, twitterings and stammerings.

As the century moved to its close, a shift of sensibility, a change in the intellectual climate made themselves felt. When the *Yellow Book* was brightening the London bookstalls, a new literary trend began to develop in Petersburg and Moscow. It went by the name of *dekadentstvo* (decadence) or modernism, eventually becoming known as symbolism. While clearly a response to a stimulus from abroad, it was also a reaction against the state of affairs at home: lack of craftsmanship in verse, the materialistic and social bias of both the Populist and Marxist branch of the intelligentsia. A rather fruitful development, though not without puerile affectations and eccentricities intended to confound the Philistine, modernism was at once a fresh beginning and a revival.

Its advent was preceded by a flourish of critical admonitions, and, indeed, throughout its existence Russian symbolism was exposed to the winds of doctrine. Its first apostle was N. Minsky. In a number of essays written in the eighties and early nineties, he championed aestheticism and amoral individualism and inveighed against the subservience of literature to the cause of political emancipation. Again, Merezhkovsky in a lengthy essay published in 1893 attacked naturalism, utilitarian aesthetics, and "deadening positivism," and called for an art mystical in content and symbolist in technique. Both looked to a poetry engaged not with the petty evils of the day, not with mere appearance, but with absolutes and ultimates—an art seeking to penetrate to the secret heart of things and glimpse eternity behind the fleeting moment. Hence the advocacy of the symbolist method: the use of language not to state or describe, but to suggest the transcendent meanings of what the senses apprehend.

Minsky represented the individualist and aesthetic elements in modernism, Merezhkovsky its religious element. The former was a philosophical poet of limited powers, the latter chiefly a prose writer. Others came to dominate the movement they had initiated. One of the leading poets of the new school was Balmont. Rather heavy-handedly and didactically he celebrated the individual exult-

6

ing in the beauty of the world and in his own freedom. "My only fatherland," he declared, "is my desert soul." One of his early collections bears the characteristic title *Let Us Be Like the Sun* (1902). Besides the lyrics in which he sought to capture elusive moods, this spontaneous, all-too facile, all-too-prolific poet wrote hymns to the elements, poems about colors, children's verse, retold exotic myths and adapted folksongs and spells. Skill with rhythm and tone color saves little of his verse from vacuity. Occasionally it tends toward the incantatory. Not for nothing did he develop the thesis, in a turgid essay published in 1915, that poetry is in essence magic.

Brusov, too, worked the vein that Minsky had opened. Like Balmont, he was "a Narcissus of the ink bottle," but of a deliberate and cerebral temperament. In an early lyric he advised the young poet to sympathize with no one, to love only himself and to worship art alone. He scandalized the critics and the public in various ways, not least by flaunting an unprecedented eroticism, and his verse was an object of ridicule. Eventually, however, it found acceptance and by 1904 he was the acknowledged head of the symbolist school. The poet was also a scholar, and his researches led him to rediscover or reevaluate certain forgotten or neglected figures in Russia's literary past. Thus he claimed Tyutchev as one of the ancestors of the symbolists. He also contributed to new appreciation of the genius of Pushkin.

At the beginning of his career Brusov had written:

> I love all dreams, all words are dear to me
> To every god I dedicate a verse.

Later he affected the vatic pose. He was, however, neither a visionary nor an impressionist, but rather a conscious craftsman, indeed a virtuoso, with a feeling for the abstract and the typical. He was perhaps most successful in his evocations of the world of antiquity, but he was also, curiously enough, capable of dealing with social and patriotic themes, and like one of his masters, Verhaeren, found rhythms for the voices of the modern city. When he peered into the future, he beheld a dehumanizing mechanical progress and the descent of barbarians who would destroy the old civilization but

7

to whom nevertheless he extended a somewhat ambiguous welcome.

Balmont and Brusov impressed themselves forcibly on the imagination of their contemporaries at the turn of the century. Another notable poet who should be grouped with the elder symbolists was Fyodor Sologub. No less prolific than the two writers just mentioned, he lacked their versatility. He came closest to being a *décadent* of Baudelaire's stripe. There is something uncannily obsessive, if not perverse, about his work. It is weighted down with melancholy and *taedium vitae* and conveys the impression that life here below is what Dostoevsky called "the Devil's vaudeville," when it is not a dismal menagerie. From his "tormenting fatherland" he escapes into "a valley of dreams," a fair world of his own imagining. Thence the sick and humorless fantast emerges only to utter threats to the sun, prayers to Satan, hymns to Death, the Deliverer. There are moments, however, when earthly existence presents itself to the poet as a rung of "an endless ladder of perfections." Yet his hosannas are less compelling than his blasphemies.

As has been seen, from the first the advocates of the new poetry envisaged it as offering the intoxicant of mysticism to the soul weary of positivist teetotalism. There is an unmistakable religious strain in Merezhkovsky's verse, but neither Balmont nor Brusov was much of a mystic, though they readily employed religious symbols, while Sologub was inclined toward the inverted religiosity that takes the form of diabolism. It was only in the early years of the new century that there appeared within the symbolist fold several somewhat younger poets whose otherworldliness had the private and ecstatic character associated with authentic mysticism.

Chief among them were Vyacheslav Ivanov, Andrey Belyi, and Alexander Blok. The elder symbolists drew their inspiration from French poetry. Indeed, the first issue of a miscellany entitled *Russian Symbolists,* which appeared in Moscow in 1894, consisted largely of translations of Verlaine, Mallarmé, Rimbaud. The newcomers, on the other hand, responded warmly to German philosophy, Dostoevsky's mysticism, and the ideas of Vladimir Solovyov. The latter, a lay theologian, was a visionary who had believed in the imminent second coming of Christ and had written lyrics of soaring spirituality. The influence of his teachings was felt particularly by Belyi and a group of that poet's friends in Moscow. The supersensuous and the transcendental had a genuine reality for the younger symbolists. The word, declared Ivanov, is "the cryptogram of the ineffable," and symbolism, according to Belyi, "a system of mystical experience." To Brusov art was autonomous and self-sufficient and symbolism merely a literary method, distinct alike from scientific cognition and mystic intuition. Ivanov and Belyi subjected art to the ends of man's spiritual renewal and held that its ultimate meaning was religious. Poetry, they believed, was an austere theurgic activity implying a tense vigil, a waiting upon the miracle of contact with the ideal world, and the projection of that experience in symbol or myth. It was allied not so much with literature as with music, since this art was closest to the inexpressible.

If pure aestheticism was called in question, so was the cult of the ego, which had inspired the modernist revolt. Chulkov, it is true, reaffirmed the principle of personality, championing "mystical anarchism": the quest for ultimate freedom. But individualism was now regarded as leading to a desperate and perilous isolation. The concept of community (*sobornost*) loomed large in Ivanov's thinking. His verse, he said, was the carven crystal chalice of collective religious consciousness. A doctrinaire fury raged in the coteries and cliques. The air quivered with apocalyptic expectations, and words like "mystery," "abyss," "the infinite" were as cheap as turnips. Symbolism tended to become a faith, a pattern of behavior. Nowhere else does literature seem to impose itself on life as in Russia, the word becoming, as Blok put it, either bread or a stone.

The symbolists fastidiously avoided the obvious and the crude in emotion and thought, and were too absorbed in their private visions to care whether they achieved communication. There is a certain aristocratic cast to their work and not a little of it is caviar to the general. This is certainly true of Ivanov's verse. It suffers from over-refinement and abstraction and is obscured by abstruse erudition. Yet there is a clear loveliness about a few of his lyrics, including some of the many poems cast in the Grecian mold. (The soul of a

9

Hellene lived in the breast of this high priest of Russian symbolism.) Others burn with a pure spiritual flame.

Belyi too was a hieratic poet, but one who was puckish at times, a mystagogue who could be ironical about his teachings. At first his palette was gold and azure, then somber tones invaded his work, but the shadows were banished by the light of "the spiritual science," theosophy. All he had ever written, he said in a foreword to one of his late books—he was an incorrigible preface writer—formed a connected whole, the tenor of which was "a quest for truth." Sometimes this quest is conducted in a fashion too abstract and cryptic to promote the enterprise. He had as well a tendency toward extravagant, synesthetic, explosive imagery, yet he could restrain it sufficiently to write lilting ballads in the folk manner and to engage successfully in rococo stylization. His weakness for verbal innovations allies him with the futurists. Above all, he was a master of language in its purely aural aspects. None of his fellow symbolists took so much to heart the idea that poetry moves toward music. He began by writing "symphonies," pieces in cadenced prose elaborated in the style of musical compositions, and even after he turned to more conventional verse, his interest in the musical texture of his poems remained paramount.

Another, and greater, poet associated with the symbolist school, was Blok. The lyrics collected in his first book have a singular unity of mood and tone. They have their being in an atmosphere of "astral dreams," of worship and meditation, of tense waiting upon mystic illumination. Only occasionally does a harsh note rend the enchanted air and the cloven hoof flash upon the sight. Many of the pieces are love poems, but the object of the youthful poet's passion, the Lady Beautiful, is almost pure spirit, a transcendental archetype, an unearthly vision. There is something rarefied to the point of otherworldliness about the sensuality that tinges his adoration and longing, though forebodings of tragic estrangement are not lacking.

The senses assert themselves in the subsequent cycles of poems. The white melody is muffled by the dark voices of earth. Blok is still capable of producing a lyric instinct with a childlike faith, but prayer and ecstasy are now largely supplanted by irony and despair.

10

The poet descends from the empyrean. He takes cognizance of his physical surroundings, and the city with its fogs and fevers looms up in his pages. Eventually he will become aware of his age, his country, his civic responsibilities. The political upheaval of 1905–1906 may have had something to do with this transformation. More probably, it was the result of the natural growth of an artist needing contact with the tangible world inhabited by creatures of flesh and blood.

Be that as it may, the poet faces the mystery of evil. His Lady undergoes a degrading metamorphosis. She has become the temptress, the traitress, the harlot. Is she not also cosubstantial with Russia? And is not Russia's martyrdom strangely identical with his own and with Christ's? The poet is indeed stretched upon the cross of passion, but he is not entirely centered on his own distresses. His lyrics are haunted with forebodings of public disaster, of a storm that will lay waste our culture. As mankind moves closer to the catastrophe of the First World War, this sense of doom grows keener. Europe's life seems to him to be "a butterfly near a candle." Yet one thing sustains him: his faith in the Russian masses. His country inspires him with a profound emotion, compact of love and loathing and not without chauvinistic overtones. With this goes an undiluted hatred of bourgeois civilization. Nevertheless he can anticipate hopefully the industrialization of Russia, its transformation into "a new America." A realistic vein crops up in his work. He has moments of impatience with symbolism, of distaste for whatever smacks of mysticism. Yet to the end of his short life, he remained a possessed, if divided, soul, a visionary believing that at their best his poems were transcripts of silent music coming from "other worlds."

Blok, like Belyi, looked to music as the ideal goal of his art. The imagination of both was largely auditory, and one gets the impression that they tended to perceive things in terms of sound and color rather than form. Voloshin's verse, on the contrary, points to a visual imagination. Indeed, he was a painter by profession, a disciple of the French impressionists. As a poet, too, he owed much to the French. His lyrics have something of the intense colors and the plasticity of Heredia, one of the poets from whom, he said, he had

11

learned the art of verse. Like Heredia, he was an expert sonneteer. But this Parnassian had much in common with the symbolists. He rejected the raw stuff of experience, save as transmitted through one of the arts or transfigured by faith. A solitary figure, he remained aloof from literary coteries, and neither the revolution of 1905 nor the World War dislodged him from his ivory tower.

While the best talents gravitated toward the symbolist school, there were poets who remained *extra muros*. The most important of them was Ivan Bunin. When as a young man he first came upon the modernists, he described them as "sick boys with complete chaos in their heads." He was himself a traditionalist in an age of innovations, a realist in a neoromantic generation, a sober man among the God-intoxicated. His lyrics offer landscapes and neat genre pictures, they evoke the melancholy charm of vanished things and are touched with a nostalgia for the distant. A strong exotic strain fills his work with Oriental color, fragrance, and warmth. A reflective or religious note may occur in his lyrics without blurring their outlines. At their best they are examples of economy and precision.

Shortly before World War I a revulsion against the spirit that informed symbolism began to take shape. The January, 1913, issue of *Apollon*, a leading *avant-garde* review, carried two essays which were in the nature of a manifesto of a new literary trend, acmeism. Its adherents were banded together in an association which they called The Guild of Poets to underscore their workmanlike concern with a métier, rather than with anything smacking of the oracular or the sacerdotal. Believing that symbolism had seen its day, the acmeists claimed to be its rightful heirs and assigns. They appreciated what the symbolists had done to raise the standard of craftsmanship and to enrich the medium they employed. They accepted the prosodic innovations made by their elders, but they wanted to carry experimentation further. They objected to the vagueness and fluidity of the symbolist style, the prevalence of "chameleon words," and advocated the use of concrete, graphic imagery. They had a predilection for the Latin spirit, with its love of light, light that "separates objects and brings their outlines into sharp focus." They preferred a solid, tangible, visible world to a universe transformed into "a phantom," the insubstantial shadow of a higher reality.

Not that the acmeists were inclined toward naturalism. If they deplored symbolism's "fraternization with mysticism, theosophy, occultism," it was because they felt that it was lacking in piety toward the unknowable and the ineffable. In any event, they wanted to keep literature distinct from theology. Confrontation of the external world, not a plumbing of the ultimate depths of the soul; dispassionateness, not ecstasy; epigrams, not arguments; irony, not "the hopeless German seriousness cultivated by the symbolists"; a balance of the elements of poetry, not the primacy of music—such were some of the precepts of acmeism. This was, in fine, a swing toward classicism, where symbolism had strong romantic leanings and has indeed been described as neoromanticism.

The new trend was represented by several gifted poets, who had perhaps less in common than the members of the symbolist group and were also of lesser caliber. Among them was Gumilyov, founder of the Guild of Poets and spokesman for acmeism, himself a careful craftsman with a Nietzschean streak in his makeup and a weakness for exotic themes. There was also his first wife, Anna Akhmatova, a lyricist who with delicate indirection and admirable economy conveys some of a woman's more intimate responses to life. Then there were Mandelstamm and Zenkevich, each possessed of a distinctive poetic individuality, yet alike in working with a new kind of firmness and a keen sense of form. Mention should also be made of Kuzmin. Although usually identified with the symbolists, he was closer to the acmeists. He preached "beautiful clarity" and practiced poetry not as a sacred ritual, but as a "gay métier." One of the few Russian poets to experiment with free verse, he delighted in the disguises of stylization, and his fragile lyrics are marked by piquant charm and a slightly perverse sensuality.

It should be noted that the practice of the acmeists was not seldom at variance with their doctrine. Aestheticism and individualism continued to thrive among them (Mandelstamm declared that he "had never been anyone's contemporary"), and so did the tendency to retreat to remote times and strange places. In spite of the talk of a new directness, the verse of the acmeists often deals with experience at secondhand, and the demands for clarity notwithstanding, some of their poems are models of cryptic utterance.

Another postsymbolist development was futurism. Both the symbolists and their acmeist offspring spurned certain of their predecessors, but they appreciated the masters of many ages and lands, singling out for particular cultivation the writers of classical antiquity. The futurists, on the other hand, repudiated the cultural heritage lock stock, and barrel. They acknowledged no predecessors. Nor did they have anything but abuse for their contemporaries, including Marinetti and the other "Italo-futurists," from whom they stemmed. "Let us gorge ourselves with the void," one of the company cried. Academic art and Pushkin were "less intelligible than hieroglyphs" and should be jettisoned. The futurists were "new people of new life." What united them was "hatred of the past." This sentiment extended to the very language as it existed at the time of their advent. The symbolists and the acmeists after them had had a free way with language. They cultivated the inexact rhyme (rhymoid), introduced by Brusov, and occasionally used a meter (*dolnik*) which deviated from traditional prosody in being based on the principle of counting accents, not syllables. Some of them employed neologisms. The futurists declared war upon the Russian syntax, spelling, punctuation, "ordering" the public "to respect the poets' right to swell the vocabulary with arbitrary and newly coined words." They aimed at no less than elaborating a wholly new language medium for the age of the machine and the metropolis.

They expounded their credo in several manifestoes. The first of these, *A Slap in the Face of Public Taste,* which bore the signatures of Khlebnikov and Mayakovsky, appeared in 1912. It was the title piece of the second collection of futurist verse. Other such collections followed. The weird titles, the bizarre images, the grotesque juxtaposition of words—all combined to create an impression of esoteric contortionism. There was experimentation with language that came close to jabberwocky or anticipated the style of *Finnegan's Wake.* There was even juggling with patterns of syllables and

14

single letters in the manner of the *lettristes* of present-day France. On the theory that words should be used not for their intellectual signification, but for their sound and shape, a feeble attempt was made to originate "a trans-mental tongue" (*zaumnyi yazyk*), a completely private language consisting of meaningless vocables. The futurists were in the habit of giving public readings, and the more to scandalize their audiences they affected such eccentricities as boutonnières of wooden spoons, while Mayakovsky is said to have painted roses on his cheeks.

This young man's poems—five collections of them appeared between 1913 and 1917—were beginning to attract attention. There was a peculiar expressiveness about his riotous, cacophonous lines, with their bold imagery, broken rhythms, clever inexact rhymes, their mixture of the colloquial and neologistic. For all the persiflage and saucy exhibitionism in his work, it carried overtones of biting social satire and asserted fundamental humane values with Bohemian exuberance and far from Bohemian earnestness.

Another futurist, who achieved a measure of real, if brief, popularity, was Igor Severyanin. The recitals of his coy, perfumed, over-melodious verse diverted many audiences. The only thing that this dandified versifier had in common with Mayakovsky and his kind was a weakness for coined words. Their desire to raze the past he did not share. To set themselves apart from the rowdies and malcontents, Severyanin and his coterie called themselves egofuturists.

On the fringe of the futurist group was a young writer by the name of Boris Pasternak. He was repelled by its brash iconoclasm and self-vaunting, yet found its free way with words congenial. His first two books of verse, which appeared during World War I, revealed an authentic talent of great originality. He was, indeed, to develop into one of the outstanding poets of our time.

Though futurism showed a greater vitality in Russia than elsewhere, it would probably have shared the fate of a passing fashion, had it not been for the Revolution.

The establishment of the Soviet regime in November, 1917, forms the great divide in the history of Russian poetry, as in that of every

15

phase of Russian art and life. Parnassus felt the shock of the up-heaval as much as the rest of the republic of letters, though verse did manage to reach the public either in printed form or through recitals at literary gatherings, while the publication of fiction practically ceased in the general disruption. As a matter of fact, the misery and the bloodshed that marked the stormy dawn of the new era, the breakdown of the routine of living, the giant hopes and fears, the apocalyptic vision of a brave new world—all this created an atmosphere rather favorable to poetry. True, there were those among the older poets who, seeing their world crumble about them, were paralyzed by despair, or who, abhorring the objectives and methods of Bolshevism, felt called upon to oppose it. Some escaped abroad, there to eat the bitter bread of exile. Such was the case of Merezhkovsky, Balmont, Bunin, Ivanov. As the work of the expatriates was proscribed, it was effectually excluded from their country's literature. Others became exiles at home. Sologub and Kuzmin continued to write without making any concessions to the radically changed intellectual atmosphere, and soon were no longer heard from. The Revolution at last put an end to Voloshin's aloofness. During the civil war, which lasted well into 1921, he wrote lyrics instinct with exasperated and mystical patriotism and contributed to the émigré press poems that one Soviet critic denounced as "counterrevolution in verse." Voloshin ceased to be vocal a decade before his withdrawal into the final silence of the grave.

Even among the established poets there were some, however, who threw in their lot with the new regime. One of them was Brusov. The symbolist *maître* made a valiant effort to pour new wine into old bottles. In his critical essays he took to using Marxist terminology; he wrote poems on scientific themes in a materialist vein, and rather incongruously hymned Lenin, the Red Kremlin, and "the universal commune" in an erudite and hyperbolic style. Four years before his death he sealed his new allegiance by joining the Communist Party. Andrey Belyi's position was not as unequivocal. He stayed on in Russia and was not averse to collaborating with the Soviet authorities. In 1918 he brought out a lyrical sequence, *Christ Is Risen,* which the public took to be a stuttering hosanna to the

Revolution, though he was later to insist that it dealt with "very intimate personal experiences, independent of country, party, and astronomical time." This was followed by verse in his customary manner on themes wholly removed from the events of the day. In his last decade he made a further clumsy effort to move toward an acceptance of Bolshevism. He had by then abandoned verse for prose.

Alexander Blok acclaimed the Revolution with enthusiasm. He had long since come to loathe official Russia, both Church and State, and the middle-class civilization of the West repelled him equally. Mention has been made of the fact that he was haunted by forebodings of impending catastrophe. The curious thing is that the prospect of the downfall of the world in which his own being was rooted filled him with more joy than terror. He accepted the violence and destruction of revolution in the belief that it had the power to replenish the deepest sources of the people's vitality. For him, as for Andrey Belyi, the revolution was something other than a change of government or the adoption of a new system of economy. Rather was it a spiritual molting, the prelude to the creation of a new heaven and a new earth where life would be "just, clean, gay, beautiful."

It was in this mood that early in 1918, hot upon the heels of the epochal events, Blok wrote a long poem, *The Twelve*. Its full meaning was not clear to the poet himself, but it was not, he was certain, a political piece—he had a profound contempt for politics. It held, he wrote, no more than "a drop of politics." We have his word for it that while he was composing *The Twelve* and for some days afterwards, he perceived with his "physical ear a great, composite noise, the noise of the old world crashing." The poem reverberates with that harsh music. Among the writings spawned by the Revolution, *The Twelve* stands out, an enduring monument to the days that shook the world. Couched partly in a coarse ballad style new to the delicate and sophisticated lyricist, it wonderfully harmonizes its heterogeneous elements and maintains a mood of revolutionary fervor, closing triumphantly with the *non sequitur* of religious apotheosis.

17

The Twelve was promptly followed by *The Scythians*, in which the poet assumes the unaccustomed role of one who speaks in the name of his people, and which was a response to the threat of foreign intervention. In the three years that remained to him he said nothing further in verse. He seems to have lost faith in the Revolution. His mentality was wholly at variance with that which was beginning to assert itself in Soviet Russia. A few months before his death he made this entry in his diary: "The louse has conquered the whole world, that's already an accomplished fact." He foresaw changes, but all in the wrong direction, and he was well aware of the dangers to literature that lurked in the new regime. In his last public address, delivered in February, 1921, on the anniversary of Pushkin's death, he sounded a prophetic warning against the bureaucrats who were "preparing to direct poetry into channels of their own, attempting upon its secret freedom and preventing it from accomplishing its mysterious purpose." Nevertheless, Blok's works are reprinted in Russia and accorded praise as one of the glories of Soviet letters.

Two weeks after Blok's death Gumilyov was executed for participation in a conspiracy against the Soviet government. The attempt to revive the Guild of Poets, which was made in 1920, proved futile. With few exceptions—Zenkevich is one—the acmeists failed to reorient themselves in the new society, with its changed demands on literature. Anna Akhmatova, her powers at their highest, clung to her intimate, occasionally backward-looking art. After 1924 her name disappeared from the public prints until the recent war. Mandelstamm, who had gone on writing in his aloof, cryptic vein, also fell silent, and for good. Acmeism, which a Soviet critic has recently described as "a Petersburg disease," was no more.

Other trends developed. The early years of the Soviet era witnessed a proliferation of literary schools and cliques, which kept forming and reforming their ranks and fighting among themselves. Before 1924 there appeared on the scene, among others, imagists, expressionists, biocosmists (they issued their program from a *creatorium*), luminists, nothingists (*nichevoki*), form-librists, neoclassicists, fuists, constructivists. Each splinter group claimed to speak

18

for the poetry of the age. Most of them had only a shadowy existence on the lunatic fringe of literature and produced little more than pretentious and often unintelligible manifestoes.

The imagists and constructivists were the exception. The latter began by repudiating all art as passive and so unsuitable to a society in process of drastic transformation. Eventually they reconciled themselves to the idea of producing literature, that is, chiefly verse. They sought to ground it on science and technology, to saturate it with the here-and-now, to raise its potential of effectiveness to a point where it could be a real factor in the building of a socialist culture. The moving spirit of this group was a poet of considerable originality and inventiveness, who has since given up all theorizing: Ilya Selvinsky. His talent thrived in the atmosphere of experimentation and seemingly unlimited possibilities that prevailed when the Revolution was young. One of the things he attempted was to inject elements of prose into his poems. Some of these have an epic sweep, others are cast in a dramatic mold.

At one time the group included another very gifted writer: Eduard Bagritzky. He moved from a highly individualistic lyricism to verse that found its inspiration in the cause of communism. From pieces suggested by the work of futurists and Gumilyov's exotic lyrics, he turned to Soviet propaganda when the civil war reached his native Southwest. Though his themes were not confined to matters of public interest, to the end of his short life he remained a poet of the Revolution, his devotion to the cause going beyond ideological allegiance. Nevertheless he clung with uncompromising tenacity to his private vision of the world, and as a result his tense, full-blooded poetry is not seldom unwarrantably obscure. Nikolay Tikhonov's more accessible verse followed much the same path.

The imagists, who had no link with the Anglo-American group of that name, tried to outdo the futurists in the choice of striking metaphors, but they also preached the poet's duty to romanticize and idealize life. In fact, between 1922 and 1924, when the confraternity dissolved, their rallying point was a meager review that flaunted the title: *A Hostelry for Travelers in the Beautiful.* The group included several minor versemakers, notably Marienhof, and one important

19

poet: Sergey Yesenin. This half-educated village lad had a fresh and authentic, if brittle, talent, but he did not quite fulfil the rich promise of his youth. His work is rooted in his rural background, and so in a class-conscious age he and several other writers of similar origin were lumped together as peasant poets. These were by no means simpleminded rustics who composed their songs as they followed the plow, but they did operate with the details of the peasant's life and faith, drawing upon immemorial folklore and the imagery of the Church books that for so long were the sole reading matter of the masses.

Yesenin greeted the coming of the new order ecstatically. To him, as to Kluyev, the other noted peasant poet who was Yesenin's senior, the Revolution was a mammoth *Jacquerie,* an elemental conflagration. They hoped that out of the ashes a muzhik Utopia would rise. The unfolding of events could not but disillusion them. Anticipating the urbanization and industrialization of the country, which he blessed in spite of the fact that this doomed his world, Yesenin decided that he was "the last poet of the village." Thus there was a semblance of logic in his suicide. Posthumous selections from his work have been repeatedly issued under Soviet imprints, but the critics have not hesitated to brand him and also Kluyev and Oreshin as kulak poets.

In addition to the groups enumerated above, there were the futurists. They embraced the revolutionary cause from the first. While others were hostile or hung back, these young Bohemians leaped to the support of the new regime. They, too, were for a complete break with the past, were they not? Obviously they could provide an appropriate literature for the victorious proletariat. Not without some misgivings the Bolsheviks welcomed this ally. As the term futurism trailed unsavory associations, it was rejected, in 1923, in favor of LEF (Left Front of the Arts). Marxist critics had much to object to in LEF's theory and practice, but they gave their unqualified approval to the work of its leader, Mayakovsky.

He was becoming a towering figure. Under the new dispensation he curbed his weakness for the bizarre and the extravagant, without, however, giving up all his odd ways with words, and stepped, as he put it, on the throat of his song. He made himself the loud-speaker, in more senses than one, of the Revolution. He hymned it, he composed marching songs for it, he eulogized Lenin and the Party, "the million-fingered hand clenched in a crushing fist"; he vociferated against the enemies of the Soviets. He applied himself also to more prosaic labors. There was no task too mean for him. He wrote poems urging his fellow citizens to brush their teeth and, also for the sake of hygiene, to refrain from handshaking, to visit the new Moscow planetarium, patronize communal restaurants, observe fire regulations, refrain from celebrating Easter. He wrote advertisements for the State department stores and denounced the State mills for the poor quality of the socks they turned out. By his own account, he produced six thousand rhymed slogans, which appeared on posters, three thousand of them painted by himself, or were used in other ways—on candy wrappers, for instance. "I am not a poet," he wrote in 1927, "but first of all a man who has put his pen at the service, mind you—the service, of the present hour, the immediate actuality and its forgers: the Soviet government and the Party." He wielded his powerful pen now as a weapon, now as a tool, always in fulfilment of what LEF theoreticians called "a social assignment." His verse, with its posteresque crudities, its oratorical exuberance, its raucousness and didacticism, was a complete denial of the graces, the subtleties, the intimacies of the poetry of the age that lay behind him.

Though his thrusts at the bureaucrats, the pedants, the parasites—he was capable of vitriolic satire—won him many enemies, Mayakovsky came to have a great vogue. It is a matter for conjecture what drove this sanguine yea-sayer to take his own life at the height of his powers. He had publicly condemned suicide when five years previously Yesenin had destroyed himself. Posthumously he was enshrined as the poet laureate of the regime. Most of the comment on his writing is in the nature of homilies on a text allegedly supplied, in 1935, by Stalin himself: "Mayakovsky was and remains the most talented poet of our Soviet epoch, and an indifferent attitude to his memory and his works is a crime."

21

In striking contrast to the work of Mayakovsky is that of a friend of his youth, Boris Pasternak, who has already been mentioned. Pasternak, too, accepted the Revolution and the regime that it fathered. He even attempted to deal with themes having obvious political implications, as in the long poem about Lieutenant Schmidt who headed a naval mutiny in 1905. Yet he has not felt it incumbent upon him to celebrate the new faith or to persuade anyone of its merits. In a day and a generation that demand from poetry, as from the other arts, participation and, indeed, partisanship, he has managed to remain above the battle. He has clung to an idealistic aestheticism in a society which has conferred official status on the materialistic outlook. He went further: he hinted that poetry with its concern for what is unique in the individual is incompatible with collectivism, the triumph of which, in fact, dooms "the winged rightness" of art.

His verse deals with a narrow range of ordinary things and not unusual situations: a summer rain, a sunrise, a mountain landscape, a thaw, an incident in an intimate personal relationship. Yet it is poles removed from conventional, rational discourse. It is a kind of shorthand, which not infrequently defies transcription. Pasternak makes no attempts to coin words, and his rhythmic patterns are by no means new, nor is his virtuosity with tone color unique. What gives his style its individuality is the phrasing, the sequences, the juxtaposition of words, suggesting a common denominator to most heterogeneous elements, indeed implying that all things are interchangeable. His is a highly studied style, dense and opaque, the vehicle of an inbred, elliptical, idiosyncratic mode of thinking. In trying to follow it the mind is severely strained, but also exhilarated. To find work in English suggestive of Pasternak's, one must turn to the performance of such a poet as Dylan Thomas. Pasternak's metaphors are as fresh and as willful. Sometimes delightfully homely, they more often tax the imagination, demanding a difficult traffic in abstractions and causing a violent dislocation of habitual associations. Always Pasternak displays an extraordinary gift for discerning far-fetched similarities, his work thus brilliantly illustrating Wallace Stevens's definition of poetry as "a satisfying of the desire for resemblance." The total effect of exposure to Pasternak's work is at once to remove us from the actual and to intensify our sense of reality.

Another difficult poet and one addicted to technical experimentation was Marina Tzvetayeva. She shared with Pasternak the capacity for mental short-cuts which gives the impression of intellectual confusion, and, like him, she was a stammerer among the glib. The blurred impression produced by much of her work is due to an intense and uncontrolled emotionalism.

There was yet another school that enlivened the literary scene and for years dominated it: the proletarian writers. Poems and stories on working-class themes written by working-class people from a working-class viewpoint had found their way into print before the Revolution. Fifty volumes of "proletarian" verse were published between 1908 and 1915. Under the new regime this sort of writing blossomed out fully in the sun of public encouragement. From the first, proletarian writers, the majority of them versifiers, were nursed along by "Proletarian Cultural-Educational Organizations" (Proletcults), which had originated shortly before the October Revolution. They issued books and magazines, and set up classes, seminars and studios where poetry and the other arts were taught and practiced and which attracted not only beginners but people whose work had already seen publication.

The number of Proletcults kept growing and their prospects seemed bright, but their heyday was brief. Their leaders argued that since there was an unbreakable nexus between art and the class struggle, the literature of the new age could be created only by writers who were flesh of the flesh and bone of the bone of the revolutionary vanguard, the industrial workers. This was a plausible Marxist thesis. But these ideologists had the temerity to claim for the organization immunity from Party control. The Party rejected this claim at Lenin's instigation. He, for one, preferred the development along socialist lines of the best elements in the bourgeois culture. Other influential Communists, notably Trotzky, on theoretical grounds denied the very possibility of a proletarian culture. In December, 1920, the Proletcults were placed under the Commissariat of Education and made subject to the directives of the Central Committee of the Party. This was the start of their decline and by 1922 they were definitely on the way out. In this downfall their detractors saw, not without reason, the collapse of an attempt to produce culture in a retort, under laboratory conditions remote from the actualities of Soviet life.

Long before the activities of the Proletcults came to a standstill, associations of proletarian writers had sprung up outside those organizations. The first of these groups, The Smithy, was formed in 1920 and had a membership of predominantly working-class background, which included some Proletcult nurslings. Two years later there came into existence another confraternity, which took the name October, sacred to revolutionary memories, and which consisted in part of secessionists from The Smithy. Both groups had their headquarters in Moscow. Similar associations arose in Leningrad and in the provinces. They warred with each other and issued rival manifestoes, much like their despised nonproletarian confrères. Nevertheless, in 1925 these bodies managed to set up an All-Russian Association of Proletarian Writers. By that time they had given up any claim to immunity from Party control.

Early proletarian verse gave expression to a mood of exultation. It celebrated the might and glory of the working class, the joy of collective labor freed from exploitation, Russia as "the mother of Soviets" rocking "the cradle of beautiful centuries." Steel, concrete, electricity were glorified in hyperbolic rhetoric, and so was the machine, "the iron Messiah." With the millennium seemingly at the door and man about to move mountains and command the stars, why should not a poet urge revolution on a global, indeed on a planetary scale? Several Leningrad proletarian versifiers banded together as cosmists. One poem urged the erection of a "Palace of World Freedom" beside the canals of Mars.

The retreat from socialism signalized by the New Economic Policy, inaugurated at the end of the civil war, had a sobering effect. Mikhail Gerasimov, for one, sounded a bitter note in a poem, suggesting that NEP was a betrayal of the Revolution. But such kill-joys were few and far between. As reconstruction got under way, the

24

scene was increasingly dominated by poets, many of them proletarian in name only, who did not question the wisdom of the Party and took every occasion to proclaim their devotion to communism. Mostly sanguine young people who had become articulate since the Revolution, they employed a realistic style and were engrossed in such matters as production costs and the state of the currency. Distrustful of lyricism, they were developing a penchant for rhymed narratives. While recently Balmont and Brusov, as well as Verhaeren and Walt Whitman, had been the poets' models, now it was Mayakovsky, though some preferred conventional meters to his irregular cadences. Straightforward propaganda, like that turned out for the dailies by the indefatigable Demyan Bednyi, gains in comparison with the more ambitious, if uninspired, performance of most of his fellows. A few purveyors of verse rose above the general level of mediocrity: Gerasimov, mentioned above, Gastev, Poletayev, Kazin, Bezymensky. Except for Gastev, whose interest in writing was short-lived, they did not confine themselves to political poetry and their work showed a certain amount of technical competence in addition to individuality.

When the first Five-Year Plan was launched in 1928, the poets, like other soldiers of the pen, applied themselves dutifully to the task of promoting industrialization and rural collectivization. Alexander Tvardovsky, a newcomer of genuine talent, first gained distinction with a long narrative poem on the subject of collective farming. Verse, however, was by this time quite overshadowed by fiction and semifictional reportage. The literary schools which had added to the stir and excitement of the early twenties now folded up and the factional fury abated. The distinction between proletarian and nonproletarian (fellow traveler) writing lost its meaning, and in 1932 the Party abolished the Association of Proletarian Writers on the ground that the authors had achieved an ideological homogeneity which made its existence unnecessary. It was replaced by a single all-embracing Union of Soviet Writers, which is still functioning. According to its statutes, members aim at "the creation of works of high artistic significance, permeated by the heroic struggle of the international proletariat and by exultation

25

over the victory of socialism, and reflecting the great wisdom and heroism of the Communist Party."

Efforts to startle and waylay the public had ceased, and the trend now was toward simple, accessible, obvious verse, innocent of irony and paradox, eschewing eccentricities of style and all experimentation. In addition to conventional lyrics and variations on the inexhaustible theme of the civil war, many poems were written in connection with and in furtherance of specific Soviet policies. There were pieces that carried a patriotic message and extolled stubborn strength and readiness to bear the brunt of battle; that paid homage to the heroism of the pilot, Chkalov, and the labors of Michurin, the Russian Burbank; there were encomiums to Lenin and more particularly to Stalin. The era of writing with a made-to-order look was in full swing. Few of the poets who had lent luster to the first dozen years of the Soviet period had survived. The newcomers, like Shchipachev, were of lesser stature. The thin sheaf of poems, under the promising title, *Second Birth,* brought out by Pasternak in 1932, did not justify the hopes of the critics that he would fall in line with his colleagues, nor did it show notable advance in the development of his authentic, if narrow, talent. He has done little original work since, devoting himself largely to rendering Shakespeare, Shelley, Keats into Russian. Other poets, notably Tikhonov, translated verse from the many languages spoken in the Union. As in the past, translation was an important function of the poet, but now its purpose was less to make world masterpieces accessible to Russian readers than to strengthen the bond that holds the various Soviet nationalities together.

"The arming of the souls of our fellow citizens with flaming love of our country and searing hatred of the enemy," the Union of Soviet Writers declared in an address presented to Stalin shortly after V–E Day, "was the content of all our work in the days of the Great Patriotic War." The versemakers' contribution to this effort bulked large. Intended to stiffen the morale of both the soldiery and the civilians, the war poetry addressed itself to the more elementary emotions in simple, direct language. Much of it was what Louis MacNeice calls "slogan poetry." A novel note was the acknowledgment of man's spiritual resources and even an appeal to religious feeling. Practically every established poet was moved to utterance by the conflict, and a number of novices, the versatile Konstantin Simonov for one, found their subject matter there. Ehrenburg, who had written some imitative verse at the beginning of his career, now returned to this medium with commendable results. Even Pasternak produced a number of war poems, in which he tried, not quite successfully, to adopt a less esoteric manner than was natural to him. Selvinsky took the same road. Anna Akhmatova's name reappeared in the public prints under a few lyrics, one of them a noble call for courage in the national emergency. In fact, the finest and most sustained war poems came from the pen of women, Margarita Aliger among them. This is all the more remarkable, since traditionally literature is man's work in Russia.

During the war official control of literature was somewhat relaxed, but at the end of hostilities the reins were tightened again. In the summer of 1946 Anna Akhmatova was expelled from the Union of Soviet Writers, which is tantamount to proscription, after having been vilified in a speech by Andrey Zhdanov, a top Party official. The charge against her was that her poems were permeated with "the spirit of pessimism and decadence." Pasternak, who had long been persona non grata with the Communists, and on one occasion had had to make a public apology for some of his lines, was denounced as a writer out of tune with Soviet literature. The old cry is now being repeated over and over again in the customary accents of authority, but with a new urgency and intransigeance: the writer's work must serve one purpose—the building of the communist order, he must hew to the Party line, unpartisan writing is not to be tolerated. Whatever is susceptible of being interpreted as influenced by, let alone expressing sympathy with, the West is excoriated by umbrageous critics. Hence, whatever shows traces of "formalism," that is, of concern with sophisticated form, is subject to attack as pointing to bourgeois corruption. And adverse criticism implies a threat to more than prestige. Where imaginative writing is held to be a political instrument, a writer's alleged errors verge on political offense.

Nevertheless, verse continues to be produced. In fact, it receives generous space in the public prints. It affects an easy, explicit style and moves in traditional metrical patterns. The one firmly entrenched technical innovation is the rhymoid (inexact rhyme), introduced by Brusov and cultivated by Blok and Mayakovsky. The latter's performance commands universal admiration, but is seldom imitated. Much that is published consists of translations of non-Russian Soviet work, and there are many occasional pieces, called forth by an anniversary, an election, a financial measure, such as the revaluation of the ruble, a speech of Stalin's. The generalissimo has been glorified so long and so fulsomely that each new paean is a real tribute—to the rhymester's inventiveness. Reminiscences of enemy atrocities in the recent war and of deeds of Soviet heroism furnish the stuff of many poems, and a favorite subject are the experiences of Red Army men in foreign parts, chiefly their homesickness. Other topics are: victory and peace; the tasks of reconstruction; the labors of the collective farmer, the miner, the steelworker, the road builder; variations on such themes as: "Our flag is the world's noblest"; "There are no people on the planet stronger and happier than we." Of late the versemakers have swelled the chorus of anti-British and particularly anti-American propaganda.

Lyrics dealing, some of them felicitously, with personal, nonpolitical subjects also find their way into print. They are apt to convey elation, and though sometimes a note of sorrow creeps in, there is scarcely ever a sign of bitterness, skepticism or irony. Indeed a patriotic optimism is one of the main specifications that poetry, in fact all literature, is expected to meet in order to produce the buoyant, energizing tonic effect that is mandatory.

In the past Russian poetry moved within the Western literary tradition. Fed by native sources, it responded readily to stimuli from France, Germany, England, and it shared their debt to classical antiquity. With the Revolution came an isolationist tendency, officially fostered. Since the end of the war the Kremlin has been making a systematic effort to segregate the country intellectually from the rest of the world. Even if that tendency had been absent, Soviet verse would have diverged widely from the poetry written in the rest of the Western world. Here poetry is currently apt to be regarded as a special way of knowing the world, while the Soviet view is that poetry should be a way of changing the world. Moreover, the Russian poet is living under an authoritarian regime which not only maintains a strict preliminary censorship over literature, but attempts, through the instrumentality of the Communist Party, to direct it in the way it should go. Like the novelists, the painters, the composers, the poets are assigned an important part in molding opinion and inspiring action. They are encouraged to take their task seriously and to plan their work with the circumspection of statesmen. But since they are not trusted, they are not accorded the freedom the creative artist requires. They are expected to work in conformity with a ready-made ideology under the Party's guidance and in furtherance of its policies.

The latter part of the present book shows that nevertheless poetry has survived under this regime. Some of the recent verse, particularly that written by young people, has a spirited, virile quality, grounded, it would seem, in the poet's sense of identity with the group. Yet it is difficult to be sanguine regarding the outlook of literature as a free art in a society that is no more able to tolerate a laissez-faire policy in cultural matters than in other areas. Even poetry, the least ideological and so the least vulnerable of the literary forms, must suffer in an atmosphere of official suspicion, repression, and dictation. Years ago a French painter had some apposite words to say on the subject. In 1870 Gustave Courbet wrote:

The State is incompetent where art is concerned. When it undertakes to reward, it usurps the role of the public taste. Its interference is wholly demoralizing—fatal to the artist, to whom it gives a false notion of his importance, fatal to art, which it constrains within the bonds of what is officially considered proper, and which it condemns to the most sterile mediocrity; the wise thing for the State is to keep hands off. The day on which it leaves us free is the one on which it will have fulfilled its duty toward us.

Gavriil Derzhavin

ON THE EMPEROR'S DEPARTURE, DECEMBER 7, 1812 °

Lo, my prophetic dreams are very truth at last:
France bows to Russia's might and Europe is laid low.
The glory we may claim no nation yet surpassed!
The gift of peace 'tis in our power to bestow.
Be the Greek Alexander renowned as great in war,
But who brings peace on earth, his soul is greater far!

[1812]

° On that day Alexander I, receiving word that the Russian army had entered Vilna, left the capital for Kutuzov's headquarters to hearten the troops by his presence.

"TIME'S LONG AND EVER–FLOWING RIVER" °

Time's long and ever-flowing river
To all men's works a finis brings,
And in the great gulf of oblivion
Drowns realms and peoples and their kings.
And if the voice of lyre and trumpet
Hold aught awhile above the spate,
That too eternity will swallow,
That too endure the common fate.

[1816]

° Derzhavin's last lines, penned three days before his death.

Vasily Zhukovsky

REMEMBRANCE

How many dear companions who enlivened for us
The world's rough road are gone, each fellow traveler
   Much missed; yet say not sadly: they have left us!
   But rather say, with gratitude: they were.

                    [*1821*]

Dmitry Venevitinov

FATHERLAND *

How ugly nature is here, truly:
Fields whose meek flatness gives offense
(It seems the very land in Russia
Takes height as an impertinence);
Mean huts and taverns; bare legs taking
Big-bellied wenches on their way;
Poor peasants shod with bast that's rotting;
Roads that facilitate delay;
And steeples, oh, what endless steeples—
Enema tubes in effigy;
And wretched views from manor houses
Of landscaping bizarrerie;
Filth, vileness, stench, cockroaches swarming,
The knout supreme on every hand—
And that is what our countless boobies
Keep calling, "sacred Fatherland."

[1826] 1924

* There is some doubt as to the authenticity of this poem, discovered
nearly a century after it was written.

Kondraty Ryleyev

CITIZEN

Am I the one who in these fateful days
Will tarnish the proud name of citizen,
And ape your wanton ways, degenerate Slavs,
You who no longer are a race of men?
Nay, I cannot deliver up my youth
To idleness, the arms of lust I flee,
My fiery spirit will not tolerate
The heavy shackles of autocracy.
Let feckless youths who have misread their fate,
Blind to the struggle that is drawing nigh,
Be unprepared at the heroic hour
When for man's freedom we must act or die.
Let such as those with chill indifference
Look on their country's anguish, nor foresee
Their shameful portion in the time to come,
The just reproaches of posterity.
They will repent when, rising in revolt,
The people strive to break the ancient chain
And seek among these slothful libertines
A Brutus, a Riego—but in vain.

[1825] 1861

Alexander Pushkin

TO CHAADAYEV

Not long we basked in the illusions
Of love, of hope, of tranquil fame;
Like morning mist, like dreams' delusions,
Youth's pastimes vanished as they came.
But still, with strong desires burning,
Beneath oppression's fearful hand,
The bidding of the fatherland
We are impatiently discerning;
In hope, in torment, we are turning
Toward freedom, wishing she were near,
As a young lover waits his dear
And looks and longs, consumed with yearning.
While freedom fires the blood, and now
While honor summons us—O hear it!
Friend, to our country let us vow
The noble strivings of the spirit.
Comrade, believe: joy's star will leap
Upon our sight, a radiant token;
Russia will rouse from her long sleep;
And where autocracy lies, broken,
Our names shall yet be graven deep.

[*1818*]

TO N. N.

From Aesculapius escaping,
I'm lean and shaven, but alive;
His cruel paw no more torments me,
And there is hope that I may thrive.
Now health, the light friend of Priapus,

35

And sleep, are entering my door,
And in my plain and crowded corner
Repose becomes my guest once more.
Then humor this poor convalescent,
You, too—he longs to see again
Your face, you lawless carefree creature,
Parnassus' lazy citizen,
The son of Freedom and of Bacchus,
Who worships Venus piously,
A master hand at every pleasure.
From Petersburg society,
Its chilly charms, its idle bustle,
Its clacking tongues that nothing stills,
Its various and endless boredom,
I'm summoned by the fields and hills,
The shady maples in the garden,
The bank of the deserted burn,
The liberties the country offers.
Give me your hand. I shall return
At the beginning of October:
We'll drink together once again,
And o'er our cups with friendly candor
Discuss a dozen gentlemen—
We'll talk of fools and wicked gentry,
And those with flunkeys' souls from birth,
And sometimes of the King of Heaven,
And sometimes of the czar on earth.

[*1819*]

GAY FEAST

I love the festive board
Where joy's the one presiding,
And freedom, my adored,
The banquet's course is guiding;

Where "Drink!" half-drowns the song
That only morning throttles;
Where wide-flung is the throng,
And close the jostling bottles.

[1819]

GRAPES

I shall not miss the roses, fading
As soon as spring's fleet days are done;
I love the grapes whose clusters ripen
Upon the hillsides in the sun—
The glory of my fertile valley,
They hang, each lustrous as a pearl,
Gold autumn's joy, oblong, transparent,
Like the slim fingers of a girl.

[1820]

A NEREID

Below the dawn-flushed sky, where the green billow lies
Caressing Tauris' flank, I saw a Nereid rise.
Breathless for joy I lay, hid in the olive trees,
And watched the demigoddess ride the rosy seas.
The waters lapped about her swan-white breast and young,
As from her long soft hair the wreaths of foam she wrung.

[1820]

THE COACH OF LIFE

Though often somewhat heavy-freighted,
The coach rolls at an easy pace;
And Time, the coachman, grizzly-pated,
But smart, alert, is in his place.

We board it lightly in the morning
And on our way at once proceed;
Repose and slothful comfort scorning,
We shout: "Hey, there! Get on! Full speed!"

Noon finds us done with reckless daring,
And shaken up. Now care's the rule.
Down hills, through gulleys roughly faring,
We sulk, and cry: "Hey, easy, fool!"

The coach rolls on, no pitfalls dodging.
At dusk, to jolts more wonted grown,
We drowse, while to the night's dark lodging
Old coachman Time drives on, drives on.

[1823]

"WITH FREEDOM'S SEED" *

"Behold, a sower went forth to sow."

With freedom's seed the desert sowing,
I walked before the morning star;
With pure and guiltless fingers throwing—
Where slavish plows had left a scar—
The living seed that should have quickened,
But hope, at last grown weary, sickened
To learn how sad lost labors are. . . .
Graze if you will, you peaceful nations,
Who never rouse at honor's horn!
Should flocks heed freedom's invocations?
Their part is to be slain or shorn,
And wear the bells tame sires have worn
Through whipped and sheeplike generations.

[1823]

* In a letter dated December 1 (Old Style), 1823, Pushkin described
this poem as "an imitation of a parable by that moderate democrat,
Jesus Christ."

ON COUNT M. S. VORONTZOV *

Half hero and half ignoramus,
What's more, half scoundrel, don't forget.
But on this score the man gives promise:
He's apt to make a whole one yet.

[*1824*]

* *Pushkin's superior in Odessa.*

"THOUGH SOPORIFIC NOT A LITTLE"

Though soporific not a little,
He's so pugnacious, you would think
That with a mad dog's foaming spittle
This critic thins his opiate ink.

[*1824*]

"BENEATH HER NATIVE SKIES"

Beneath the azure of her native skies she drooped,
    To fade, to vanish past returning;
It may be the young ghost above me briefly stooped
    And swept me with a shadowy yearning.

But now between us lies a line I may not cross.
    I cannot rouse the old devotion:
Indifferent lips were those that told me of my loss,
    I learned of it without emotion.

So that is she who set my spirit all afire
    With love that mingled tender sadness
And grievous straining, weary ache of sharp desire,
    That was heart's torment and mind's madness!

39

Where is the torment now, the love? Alas, the host
    Of memories that thus outlive you
Can stir no tears, you credulous, poor ghost,
    In one with no regrets to give you.

[*1825*]

WINTER EVENING

Storm clouds dim the sky; the tempest
Weaves the snow in patterns wild;
Like a beast the gale is howling
And now wailing like a child;
On the worn old roof it rustles
The piled thatch, and then again
Like a traveler belated
Knocks upon the windowpane.

Sad and dark our shabby cottage,
Indoors not a sound is heard.
Nanny, sitting at the window,
Can't you give me just a word?
What is wrong, dear? Are you wearied
By the wind, so loud and rough?
Or the buzzing of your distaff—
Has that set you dozing off?

Let us drink, dear old companion,
You who shared my sorry start;
Get the mug and drown our troubles:
That's the way to cheer the heart.
Sing the ballad of the titmouse
That beyond the seas had gone,
Or the song about the maiden
Fetching water just at dawn.

Storm clouds dim the sky; the tempest
Weaves the snow in patterns wild;
Like a beast the gale is howling
And now wailing like a child.
Let us drink, dear old companion,
You who shared my sorry start;
Get the mug and drown our troubles:
That's the way to cheer the heart.

[1825]

THE PROPHET *

Athirst in spirit, through the gloom
Of an unpeopled waste I blundered,
And saw a six-winged Seraph loom
Where the two pathways met and sundered.
He set his fingers on my eyes:
His touch lay soft as slumber lies—
And like an eagle's, scared and shaken,
Did my prophetic eyes awaken.
He touched my ears, and lo! they rang
With a reverberating clang:
I heard the spheres revolving, chiming,
The angels in their soaring sweep,
The monsters moving in the deep,
The vines low in the valley climbing.
And from my mouth the Seraph wrung
Forth by its roots my sinful tongue,
The idle tongue that slyly babbled,
The vain, malicious, the unchaste,
And the wise serpent's sting he placed
In my numb mouth with hand blood-dabbled;
And with a sword he clove my breast,

* See Isaiah, 6 : 1–10.

Drew forth the heart that shook with dread
And in my gaping bosom pressed
A glowing coal of fire instead.

Upon the wastes, a lifeless clod,
I lay, and heard the voice of God:
"Arise, O prophet, look and ponder:
Arise, charged with my will and spurred,
The roadways and the seaways wander,
Kindling men's hearts with this, my Word."

[1826]

MESSAGE TO SIBERIA *

Deep in the Siberian mine,
Keep your patience proud;
The bitter toil shall not be lost,
The rebel thought unbowed.

The sister of misfortune, Hope,
In the under-darkness dumb
Speaks joyful courage to your heart:
The day desired will come.

* This poem is addressed to the participants in the abortive armed up-
rising against the autocracy, which occurred in December, 1825. Pushkin
handed it to the wife of one of the Decembrists who was leaving to
join her husband in Siberia. In reply to this message one of the exiles,
Prince Alexander Odoyevsky (1802–1839), wrote a poem which at one
time was very popular in revolutionary circles. In it he assured "the
bard" that the Decembrists were proud of their chains and that their
faith in the cause of freedom was unshaken:

> Our grievous labors were not all in vain:
> A flame will yet be kindled from the spark.

The last line is printed at the masthead of The Spark, the central organ
of the Russian Social Democratic Workers' Party, which in 1900–1903
was edited by Lenin abroad and smuggled into Russia.

And love and friendship pour to you
Across the darkened doors,
Even as round your galley-beds
My free music pours.

The heavy-hanging chains will fall,
The walls will crumble at a word;
And Freedom greet you in the light,
And brothers give you back the sword.

[1827] 1874

ARION

We numbered many in the ship;
Some spread the sails, some pulled, together,
The mighty oars; fair was the weather.
The rudder in his steady grip,
Our helmsman silently was steering
The heavy galley through the sea,
While I, in blithe serenity,
Sang to the crew . . . when suddenly
A rough gust swooped, the waves were rearing . . .
The helmsman and the crew were lost!
No sailor by the storm was tossed
Ashore—but I who had been singing.
I chant the hymns I sang before,
And dry my garments, wetly clinging,
Upon the sunned and rocky shore.

[1827]

THREE SPRINGS

Three springs in life's immense and joyless desert
Leap into light from a mysterious source;
The spring of youth, boiling in bright rebellion,

Bubbles and sparkles ere it runs its course;
Life's exiles at the clear Castalian fountain
Drink draughts more pure, more heady than the first;
But 'tis the deep, cold wellspring of oblivion
That slakes most sweetly ecstasy and thirst.

[1827]

REMEMBRANCE

When noisy day at last is quieted
    And on the hushed streets of the town,
Half diaphane, night's shadow lies, and sleep,
    The wage of toil, is handed down,
Then in the silence how the hours drag out
    My weary vigil; then up start
Snakes of remorse nocturnal torpor wakes
    To livelier flame that stings the heart.
Dreams surge and eddy; anguish crowds the mind
    With wounding thoughts that press too close;
In silence memory unrolls for me
    A scroll as long as it is gross;
I read and loathe the record of the years,
    And shake, and curse the grim display;
My groans are bitter, bitter are the tears
    That wash no sorry line away.

[1828]

"THE MAN I WAS OF OLD"

Tel j'étais autrefois et tel je suis encor.°

The man I was of old, that man I still remain:
Lighthearted, quick to fall in love. My friends, 'tis vain
To think I can behold the fair without elation

° *The epigraph is from* André Chénier.

44

And timid tenderness and secret agitation.
Has love not played with me and teased me quite enough?
In Cytherea's nets, wrought of such sturdy stuff,
Like a young hawk have I not struggled long and striven?
Unchastened by the pangs whereby I have been driven,
Unto new idols I my old entreaties bring. . . .

[1828]

THE UPAS TREE

In the niggard, sickly desert,
Where the earth is baked to stone,
Stands the upas, a stern sentry,
In the universe alone.

On a day of wrath did Nature,
Mother to those thirsty plains,
Bear it, saturate with poison,
Dead green leafage, roots and veins.

Through its bark the poison oozes,
Molten in noon's heat and rich,
Hardening as dusk advances
To a thick, transparent pitch.

Not a bird flies toward those branches,
Not a tiger nears; a black
Gust may briefly burst upon it:
Blight will follow in its track.

If a vagrant cloud should shower
The thick foliage where it stands,
From those boughs a rain of poison
Pours into the burning sands.

But a man a man commanded
By one look to seek that tree;
He returned, he bore the poison,
As he went, submissively.

Back he brought the mortal poison,
Withered was the branch he bore,
From his brow of deathy pallor
The chill sweat streamed evermore.

Back he brought it—drooped, and sickened,
Falling on a bed of bast;
To his mighty master faithful,
The poor slave soon breathed his last.

And the prince with that dread poison
Steeped his passive arrows well,
And sent ravage to his neighbors
And sped ruin far and fell.

[*1828*]

PORTRAIT

When she, that soul of fire, appears,
O women of the North, among you,
It is a radiant challenge flung you,
Your dull conventions, worldly fears.
She spends herself as, bright and daring,
She rushes on against those bars,
How like a lawless comet flaring
Among the calculated stars!

[*1828*]

"LOVELY YOUTH"

(Camp on the Euphrates)

Lovely youth, when war drums rattle
Be not ravished: seal your ears;
Do not leap into the battle
With the crowd of mountaineers.
Well I know that death will shun you,
And that where the sabers fly
Azrael will look upon you,
Note your beauty, and pass by.
But the war will be unsparing:
Surely you will come to harm—
Lose your timid grace of bearing,
Lose your shy and languid charm.

[1829]

"I LOVED YOU ONCE"

I loved you once, nor can this heart be quiet,
For it would seem that love still lingers here;
But do not you be further troubled by it:
I would in no wise sadden you, my dear.
I loved you without hope, a mute offender;
What jealous pangs, what shy despairs I knew!
A love as deep as this, as true, as tender,
God grant another may yet offer you.

[1829]

"HERE'S WINTER"

Here's winter. Far from town, what shall we do? I question
The servant bringing in my morning cup of tea:
"How is the weather—warm? Not storming? The ground's covered

With freshly fallen snow?" Come, is it best to be
Astride a horse at once, or shall we, until dinner,
See what the neighbor's old reviews may have to say?
The snow is fresh and fine. We rise, and mount our horses,
And trot through fields agleam with the first light of day.
We carry whips; the dogs run close behind our stirrups;
With careful eyes we search the snow, we scour the plain
For tracks, ride round and round, and tardily at twilight,
After we've missed two hares, at last turn home again.
How jolly! Evening comes: without, the storm is howling;
The candlelight is dim. The heart is wrenched with pain.
Slow drop by drop I drink my boredom's bitter poison.
I try a book. The eyes glide down the page—in vain:
My thoughts are far away . . . and so I close the volume,
Sit down, take up my pen, force my dull Muse to say
Some incoherent words, but harmony is wanting,
The sounds won't chime. . . . The devil! Where now is my sway
Over the rhyme? I can't control this curious handmaid:
The verse is shapeless, cold, so lame it cannot walk.
So I dismiss the Muse: I am too tired to quarrel.
I go into the parlor where I hear them talk
About the sugar-works, about the next election;
The hostess, like the weather, frowns, her only arts
Are plying rapidly her long steel knitting needles,
Or telling people's fortunes by the king of hearts.
What boredom! Thus the days go by, alike and lonely.
But if, while I play draughts at twilight in my nook,
Into our dreary village a closed sleigh or carriage
Should just by chance bring guests for whom I did not look:
Say, an old woman and two girls, her two young daughters
(Tall, fair-haired creatures, both), the place that was so dull,
So Godforsaken, all at once is bright and lively,
And suddenly, good heavens, life grows rich and full!
Attentive sidelong looks by a few words are followed,
There's talk, then friendly laughter, and songs when lamps are lit
And after giddy waltzes there come languid glances,

There's whispering at table, gay and ready wit;
Upon the narrow stairs a lingering encounter;
When twilight falls, a girl steals from her wonted place
And out onto the porch, bare-throated, chest uncovered—
The wind is up, the snow blows straight into her face!
But never mind! Our fair is heedless of the snowstorm.
Unhurt in northern blasts the Russian rose will blow.
How hotly burns a kiss in keen and frosty weather!
How fresh a Russian girl abloom in gusts of snow!

[1829]

"ALONG THE NOISY STREETS"

Along the noisy streets I wander,
A church invites me, it may be,
Or with mad youths my time I squander,
And still these thoughts are haunting me:

This year will fly, the next will follow
As fast, and all whom you see here
Eternity at last will swallow;
For some the hour is drawing near.

When I behold a lone oak thriving,
I think: age dooms me to decay,
This patriarch, though, will be surviving
As it survived my fathers' day.

If I caress a babe, I'm thinking:
Farewell, too soon I must make room
For you, and out of sight be sinking—
My time to fade is yours to bloom.

Each day, each year in thought addressing,
I ask in turn ere it flits past

How it will be remembered, guessing
Which shall be reckoned as my last.

And when fate strikes, where will it find me?
In battle, on the road, at sea?
Will that near valley be assigned me
Where my cold clay at home may be?

The witless body's unaffected,
Nor recks where it must rot, 'tis clear,
Yet in my heart I have elected
To lie near places once held dear.

Then, even at the grave's grim portal
Let young life play with careless grace,
And neutral Nature her immortal
Beauty spread round my resting place.

[*1829*]

TO THE POET

Poet, be deaf to popular acclaim;
The tumult of ecstatic praise will die;
The crowd's chill laughter and the dullard's blame
Thou with austere, calm firmness shalt put by.

Thou art a king. Live then alone, on high.
Take the free road thy spirit bids thee tread,
Perfect the fruit devoted thoughts have bred
And all rewards for noble toil deny.

These lie within. Thou art the highest court,
Sternest of judges, if thy work fall short.
Art thou content, exacting artist, say?

Art thou content? Then let the mob that spurns
Spit on the altar where thy fire burns,
And make thy tripod shake in childish play.

[1830]

EVIL SPIRITS

The clouds are scurrying and spinning;
The moon, in hiding, casts her light
Upon the flying snow; the heavens
Are troubled, troubled is the night.
I drive across the naked country,
The bells go ding! and ding, again!
Lonely and lost, I gaze in terror
Upon the unfamiliar plain.

"Drive faster, fellow!" "There's no help, sir,
The horses find the going rough;
The blizzard pastes my eyes together;
The roads are buried, sure enough.
There's not a track for me to follow;
We've lost our way. What shall we do?
The devil's leading us in circles
And right across the meadows, too.

"There, there he is! He's playing with us;
He spat at me, you might have seen;
He's here, befuddling the poor horses,
He'll push them into the ravine;
Now he pretends that he's a milepost
Where there was never such a mark;
He flashed by like a spark and vanished,
Vanished into the empty dark."

The clouds are scurrying and spinning;
The moon, in hiding, casts her light

Upon the flying snow; the heavens
Are troubled, troubled is the night.
We have no strength to go on circling;
The bell is silent suddenly;
The horses halt. . . . What is that yonder?
Who knows? A stump? A wolf, maybe?

The storm is vicious now, it's howling;
The nervous horses snort, oh hark!
It's he who dances in the distance,
Alone his eyes burn in the dark;
Once more the horses hurry onward,
The bells go ding! and ding, again!
Those throngs I see are evil spirits
Gathered upon the whitening plain.

Innumerable, various, horrid,
Demoniac creatures are in flight,
Whirled round like leaves in deep November
Under the wild moon's troubled light . . .
What numbers! Whither are they driven?
Their chant has such a plaintive pitch:
Is it a house sprite they are burying
Or do they marry off a witch?

The clouds are scurrying and spinning;
The moon, in hiding, casts her light
Upon the flying snow; the heavens
Are troubled, troubled is the night.
A dizzy host of swarming devils
Goes rushing through the topless sky;
It tears the heart of me to hear them,
Their desolate, long, lamenting cry.

[1830]

ON THE TRANSLATION OF THE ILIAD

Sacred, sonorous, is heard the long-muted speech of the Hellenes;
Shaken, my soul knows thee near, shade of the mighty old man.

[1830]

WORK

Here is the long-looked-for hour: the labor of years is accomplished.
Why should this sadness so vague secretly weigh on my heart?
Is it that, idle at last, I must stand like a workman unwanted,
One who has taken his pay, stranger to tasks that are new?
Is it the work I regret, the silent companion of midnight,
Friend of the aureate Dawn, friend of the gods of the hearth?

[1830]

MADONNA

Not with old masters, rich on crowded walls,
My house I ever sought to ornament,
That gaping guests might marvel while they leant
To connoisseurs with condescending drawls.
Amidst slow labors, far from garish halls,
Before one picture I would fain have spent
Eternity: where the calm canvas thralls
As though from regnant clouds the Virgin bent,
With majesty and meekness in her eyes,
The Saviour beside her, mild and wise,
Beneath the palm of Zion, these alone . . .
My wish is granted: God has shown your face
To me; here, my Madonna, you shall throne,
Most pure exemplar of the purest grace.

[1830]

ELEGY

The mirth, now dead, that once was madly bubbling,
Like fumes of last night's cups, is vaguely troubling;
Not so the griefs that to those years belong:
Like wine, I find, with age they grow more strong.
My path is bleak—before me stretch my morrows:
A tossing sea, foreboding toil and sorrows.
And yet I do not wish to die, be sure;
I want to live—think, suffer, and endure;
And I shall know some savor of elation
Amidst the cares, the woe, and the vexation:
At times I shall be drunk on music still,
Or at a moving tale my eyes will fill,
And, as sad dusk folds down about my story,
Love's farewell smile may shed a parting glory.

[1830]

"MY CRITIC"

"My critic, rosy-gilled, as quick as thought to offer
Our gloomy Muse affront, you plump, pot-bellied scoffer,
Come here, I beg, sit down, and have a little nip;
Together we may get the better of the hyp.
Behold those wretched huts: a view to feast your eyes on,
Black earth beyond, the plain that slopes toward the horizon;
Above the hovels hang low clouds, thick-massed and gray.
But the bright meadows, friend, the dark woods—where are they?
Where the blithe brook? Beside the low fence in the court
Two trees rejoice the eye; they're of a meager sort,
Such pitiable things, the two of them together,
And one is stripped quite bare by autumn's rainy weather,
The other's yellow leaves wait, sopping, to be strewn
On puddles by the wind that will be raging soon.
There's not a living cur. True, here a peasant trudges

54

Across the empty court, tagged by two kerchiefed drudges.
The coffin of a child beneath his arm, no hat
Upon his head—he calls to the priest's lazy brat
To bid his dad unlock the church—'You've legs to run with!
Be quick! We're late—high time the funeral were done with!'
Why do you frown, my friend?" "You've kept this up too long;
Can't you amuse us with a merry sort of song?"
"Where are you off to now?" "To Moscow, I am setting
Out for the birthday ball." "But are you quite forgetting
That we are quarantined? There's cholera about.
Come, cool your heels, as in the mountainous redoubt
Your humble servant did—there's nothing else to do now.
Well, brother, you don't scoff: so you've got the hyp too now!"

[1830]

"FOR ONE LAST TIME"

For one last time my thought embraces
Your image, all but lost to me;
The heart with wistful longing traces
A dream that hour on hour effaces,
And dwells upon love's memory.

Our years roll onward, swiftly changing;
They change, and we change in the end—
Far from your poet you are ranging,
And darkness like the tomb's, estranging,
Has drawn you from that passionate friend.

This heart its leave of you has taken;
Accept, my distant dear, love's close,
As does the wife death leaves forsaken,
As does the exile's comrade, shaken
And mute, who clasps him once, and goes.

[1830]

"ABANDONING AN ALIEN COUNTRY"

Abandoning an alien country,
You sought your distant native land;
How could I stop the tears at parting
When sorrow was beyond command?
With hands that momently grew colder
I tried to hold you, wordlessly
I begged that our farewells, our anguish,
Might be prolonged eternally.

But from the bitter kiss and clinging
You tore away your lips; and from
The gloomy land of lonely exile
To a new country bade me come.
You said: "When we are reunited,
Beneath a sky of endless blue,
In the soft shadow of the olives,
Then, lip to lip, I'll solace you."

But yonder, where the blue is radiant,
And where the olives from the shore
Cast tender shadows on the waters,
You fell asleep, to wake no more.
Within the funeral urn your beauty
Lies hidden with your suffering now—
But the sweet kiss of our reunion
I wait . . . I hold you to your vow.

[*1830*]

VERSES WRITTEN DURING A SLEEPLESS NIGHT

Sleepless in the dark I lie
While the earth is wrapped in slumber;
Only weary tickings number

Hours that emptily drag by.
Fate, with your glib female mutter,
Night, in sleep atwitch, aflutter,
Life, that rustles mousily,
Why will you not let me be?
What, dull whisper, are you saying—
Protest or reproach conveying
Of a day that's lost to me?
Your demands I cannot reckon;
Do you prophesy or beckon?
If your meaning I but knew!
Would that I could fathom you. . . .

[1830]

"NO, NEVER THINK"

No, never think, my dear, that in my heart I treasure
The tumult of the blood, the frenzied gusts of pleasure,
Those groans of hers, those shrieks: a young Bacchante's cries,
When writhing like a snake in my embrace she lies,
And wounding kiss and touch, urgent and hot, engender
The final shudderings that consummate surrender.
How sweeter far are you, my meek, my quiet one,
By what tormenting bliss is my whole soul undone
When, after I have long and eagerly been pleading,
With bashful graciousness to my deep need conceding,
You give yourself to me, but shyly, turned away,
To all my ardors cold, scarce heeding what I say,
Responding, growing warm, oh, in how slow a fashion,
To share, unwilling, yet to share at last my passion!

[1830]

"WHEN IN MY ARMS"

When in my arms your slender beauty
Is locked, O you whom I adore,
And from my lips in gusts of rapture
Love's tender murmurs stintless pour,
In silence from my tight embraces
Your supple form you gently free,
And with a skeptic's smile, my dear one,
You mockingly reply to me:
The sad tradition of betrayal
You have remembered all too well;
You listen with a sad indifference,
Not heeding what I have to tell. . . .
I curse the naughty zeal, the cunning,
The hot pursuit after delight
That filled my youth, the assignations,
The garden trysts in the hushed night;
I curse the whispered lovers' discourse,
The magic spells that lay in verse,
The gullible young girls' caresses,
Their tears, their late regrets I curse.

[1831]

AUTUMN

(A Fragment)

"What does not then pass through my drowsy mind?"
—Derzhavin

1.

October has arrived. The grove is shaking
The last reluctant leaves from naked boughs.
A breath of autumn cold—the road is freezing;

The millpond, glazed with ice, is in a drowse,
Though the brook babbles; with his pack my neighbor
Makes for the distant field—his hounds will rouse
The woods with barking, and his horse's feet
Will trample cruelly the winter wheat.

2.

This is my time! What is the spring to me?
Thaw is a bore: mud running thick and stinking;
Spring makes me ill: my mind is never free
From dizzy dreams, my blood's in constant ferment.
Give me instead winter's austerity,
The snows under the moon—and what is gayer
Than to glide lightly in a sleigh with her
Whose fingers are like fire beneath the fur?

3.

And oh, how jolly, on the placid river
To glide steel-shod, swiftly, with easy grace!
The shining stir of festivals in winter!
But there's a limit—nobody could face
Six months of snow—even that cave dweller,
The bear, would growl "enough" in such a case.
Sleigh rides with young Armidas pall, by Jove,
And you turn sour with loafing by the stove.

4.

Oh, darling summer, I could cherish you,
If heat and dust and gnats and flies were banished.
You dull the mind, the heart grows weary, too.
We, like the meadows, suffer drought and wither.
Drink is our only thought, and how we rue
Old woman Winter, at whose funeral banquet
Pancakes and wine were served, but now we hold
Memorial feasts of ices, sweet and cold.

5.

They say ill things of the last days of autumn:
But I, friend reader, not a one will hear;
Her quiet beauty touches me as surely
As does a wistful child, to no one dear.
She can rejoice me more, I tell you frankly,
Than all the other seasons of the year.
I am a humble lover, so I should
Find singularly much in her that's good.

6.

How shall I make it clear? I find her pleasing
As you, perhaps, may like a sickly girl,
Condemned to die, poor creature, who is drooping
And without one word of reproach to hurl
At life, forsaking her. Upon her pallid
Young lips a little smile is seen to curl.
She does not hear the grave's abysmal yawn.
Today she lives—tomorrow she is gone.

7.

Oh, mournful season that delights the eyes,
Your farewell beauty captivates my spirit.
I love the pomp of Nature's fading dyes,
The forests, garmented in gold and purple,
The rush of noisy wind, and the pale skies
Half-hidden by the clouds in darkling billows,
The early frost, the sun's infrequent ray,
And threats of grizzled Winter far away.

8.

Each time that autumn comes I bloom afresh;
For me, I find, the Russian cold is good;
Again I go through life's routine with relish;
Sleep comes in season, and the need for food;
Desire seethes—and I am young and merry,

My heart beats fast with lightly leaping blood.
I'm full of life—such is my organism
(If you will please excuse the prosaism).

9.

My horse is brought; far out onto the plain
He carries me; the frozen valley echoes
To his bright hooves with resonant refrain;
The ice creaks under him and as he gallops
In the keen wind he waves his streaming mane.
But day soon flickers out. At the forgotten
Hearth, where the fire purrs low or leaps like wind,
I read, or nourish long thoughts in my mind.

10.

And I forget the world in the sweet silence,
Imagination lulls me, and once more
The soul oppressed by the old lyric fever
Trembles, reverberates, and seeks to pour
Its burden freely forth, and as though dreaming
I watch the children that my fancy bore,
And I am host to the invisible throngs
Who fill my reveries and build my songs.

11.

And thoughts stir bravely in my head, and rhymes
Run forth to meet them on light feet, and fingers
Reach for the pen, and the good quill betimes
Asks for the foolscap. Wait: the verses follow.
Thus a still ship sleeps on still seas. Hark: Chimes!
And swiftly all hands leap to man the rigging,
The sails are filled, they belly in the wind—
The monster moves—a foaming track behind.

12.

It sails. But whither shall we sail? . . .

[*1833*]

"I VISITED AGAIN"

                      . . . I visited again
That corner of the earth where once I spent,
In placid exile, two unheeded years.
A decade's gone since then—and in my life
There have been many changes—in myself,
Who from the general law am not exempt,
There have been changes, too—but here once more
The past envelops me, and suddenly
It seems that only yesterday I roamed
These groves.

              Here stands the exile's cottage, where
I lived with my poor nurse. The good old woman
Has passed away—no longer do I hear
Through the thin wall her heavy tread as she
Goes on her busy rounds.

                    Here is the hill
Upon whose wooded crest I often sat
Motionless, staring down upon the lake—
Recalling, as I looked, with melancholy,
Another shore, and other waves I knew . . .
Among the golden meadows, the green fields,
It lies as then, that blue and spacious lake:
A fisherman across its lonely waters
Is rowing now, and dragging after him
A wretched net. Upon the sloping shores
Are scattered hamlets—and beyond them there
A mill squats crookedly—it scarcely stirs
Its wings in this soft wind. . . .

                   Upon the edge
Of the ancestral acres, on the spot
Where the rough road, trenched by the heavy rains,
Begins its upward climb, three pine trees rise—
One stands apart, and two are close together,
And I remember how, of moonlight nights,

When I rode past, their rustling greeted me
Like a familiar voice. I took that road,
I saw the pines before me once again.
They are the same, and on the ear the same
Familiar whisper breaks from shaken boughs,
But at the base, beside their aged roots
(Where everything had once been bare and bald),
A glorious young grove had risen up,
A verdant family; the bushes crowd
Like children in their shadow. And apart,
Alone as ever, their glum comrade stands,
Like an old bachelor, about whose feet
There stretches only bareness as before.
I hail you, race of youthful newcomers!
I shall not witness your maturity,
When you shall have outgrown my ancient friends,
And with your shoulders hide their very heads
From passers-by. But let my grandson hear
Your wordless greeting when, as he returns,
Content, lighthearted, from a talk with friends,
He too rides past you in the dark of night,
And thinks, perhaps, of me.

[*1835*]

"THE EREMITES OF OLD"

The eremites of old, all of the world unspotted,
That they might reach the heights to holy saints allotted,
That they might fortify the heart against life's stress,
Composed such prayers as still comfort us and bless.
But none has ever stirred in me such deep emotions
As that the priest recites at Lententide devotions;
The words which mark for us that saddest season rise
Most often to my lips, and in that prayer lies
Inscrutable support when I, a sinner, hear it:

"Oh, Lord of all my days, avert Thou from my spirit
Both melancholy sloth and poisonous love of power,
That secret snake, and joy in gossip of an hour.
But let me see my sins, O God, and not another's,
Nor sit in judgment on the lapse that is my brother's,
And quicken Thou in me the breath and being of
Forbearance and of meekness, chastity and love."

[1836]

"IN VAIN I SEEK TO FLEE"

In vain I seek to flee to Zion's lofty height:
Rapacious sin pursues, alert to watch my flight;
'Tis thus, with nostrils thrust in yielding sandy hollows,
The shy deer's pungent spoor the hungry lion follows.

[1836]

"WHEN, LOST IN THOUGHT"

When, lost in thought, I roam beyond the city's bounds
And find myself within the public burial grounds,
The fashionable tombs behind the railing squatting,
Where the great capital's uncounted dead are rotting,
All huddled in a swamp, a crowding, teeming horde,
Like greedy guests that swarm about a beggar's board;
Officials' sepulchers, and merchants', too, all fizzles:
The clumsy products of inexpert, vulgar chisels,
Inscribed in prose and verse with virtues, service, rank,
Outlandish ornaments displayed on either flank;
A widow's fond lament for an old cuckold coffined;
The posts, their urns unscrewed by thieves, the earth that's softened
And slippery, where graves are gaping dark and wide
To welcome tenants who next day will move inside—

All this brings troubled thoughts; I feel my spirits fail me
As I survey the scene, and evil blues assail me.
One wants to spit and run!
                              But what calm pleasure lies—
When rural autumn sheds its peace from evening skies—
In seeing the churchyard, where, solemnly reposing
Among their ancestors, the country dead are dozing!
There, unadorned, the graves have ample elbowroom;
At midnight no pale thief creeps forth to rob the tomb;
The peasant sighs and says a prayer as he passes
The timeworn stones o'ergrown with yellowed moss and grasses;
No noseless angels soar, no blowsy Graces here,
No petty pyramids or idle urns appear;
But a broad oak above these dignified graves brooding
Bestirs its boughs in music. . . .

[1836]

"UNTO MYSELF I REARED A MONUMENT"

Exegi monumentum

Unto myself I reared a monument not builded
By hands; a track thereto the people's feet will tread;
It raises higher than the Alexandrian pillar
    Its noble and unbending head.

I shall not wholly die—but in my songs my spirit
Will, incorruptible and bodiless, survive—
And I shall be renowned as long as under heaven
    One poet yet remains alive.

The rumor of my fame will sweep through vasty Russia,
And all its peoples speak this name that yet shall gain
Regard from Slav unborn, the Finn, the savage Tungus,
    The Kalmuck horseman of the plain.

65

For years to come the people will lovingly remember
What kindly thoughts my lyre awoke in every breast,
How in this cruel age I celebrated freedom,
    And mercy pled for those distressed.

O Muse, obey the Lord's commandments, never fearing
An insult, both to praise and blame indifferent,
Demanding no reward, sing on, and meeting folly,
    Do not descend to argument.

                        [1836]

SECULAR POWER *

When the supreme event had come to pass, and He,
Our God, upon the cross had died in agony,
On either side the tree two looked on one another:
One, Mary Magdalene, and one, the Virgin Mother—
        In grief two women stood.
But now whom do we see beneath the holy rood,
As though it were the porch of him who rules the city?
Not here the holy twain, borne down by pain and pity,
But, shakos on their heads and bayonet in hand,
Beside the crucifix two bristling sentries stand.
Are they set here to guard the cross as 'twere State cargo?
Do you fear mice or thieves? Wherefore this strict embargo?
Would you add dignity unto the King of kings?
What honor do you think your patronage thus brings,
You mighty of the earth, what help by you is rendered
To Him who's crowned with thorns, to Him who freely tendered
His body to the scourge, without complaint or fear,
The Christ who had to bear the cross, the nails, the spear?

* This poem seems to have been occasioned by the fact that when a
painting by K. P. Bryullov depicting the Crucifixion was placed on view,
sentries guarded the canvas from the press of spectators.

You dread the mob's affront to Him who won remission
Of sins, and saved the race of Adam from perdition?
Is it to keep the way for strolling gentry clear
That thus the common folk are not admitted here?

[1836] 1870

"'TIS TIME, MY FRIEND"

'Tis time, my friend, 'tis time! For rest the heart is crying.
The days go swiftly by, hour after hour flying
Bears off some shred of life—yet still we wish to live,
Though death must come, how soon? And joy is fugitive.
Not happiness, but peace and freedom may be granted
On earth: this is my hope, who by one dream am haunted—
A weary slave, I plan escape before the night
To the remote repose of toil and pure delight.

[1836]

From EUGENE ONEGIN

Tatyana's Letter to Onegin

I write you; is my act not serving
As an avowal? Well I know
The punishment I am deserving:
That you despise me. Even so,
Perhaps for my sad fate preserving
A drop of pity, you'll forbear
To leave me here to my despair.
I first resolved upon refraining
From speech: you never would have learned
The secret shame with which I burned,
If there had been a hope remaining
That I should see you once a week

Or less, that I should hear you speak,
And answer with the barest greeting,
But have one thing when you were gone,
One thing alone to think upon
For days, until another meeting.
But you're unsociable, they say,
The country, and its dullness, bore you;
We . . . we don't shine in any way,
But have a hearty welcome for you.

Why did you come to visit us?
Here in this village unfrequented,
Not knowing you, I would not thus
Have learned how hearts can be tormented.
I might (who knows?) have grown contented,
My girlish dreams forever stilled,
And found a partner in another,
And been a faithful wife and mother,
And loved the duties well fulfilled.

Another! . . . No, my heart is given
To one forever, one alone!
It was decreed . . . the will of Heaven
Ordained it so: I am your own.
All my past life has had one meaning—
That I should meet you. God on High
Has sent you, and I shall be leaning
On your protection till I die. . . .
I saw you in my dreams; I'd waken
To know I loved you; long ago
I languished in your glance, and oh!
My soul, hearing your voice, was shaken.
Only a dream? It could not be!
The moment that I saw you coming,
I thrilled, my pulses started drumming,
And my heart whispered: it is he!

Yes, deep within I had the feeling,
When at my tasks of charity,
Or when, the world about me reeling,
I looked for peace in prayer, kneeling,
That silently you spoke to me.
Just now, did I not see you flitting
Through the dim room where I am sitting,
To stand, dear vision, by my bed?
Was it not you who gently gave me
A word to solace and to save me:
The hope on which my heart is fed?
Are you a guardian angel to me
Or but a tempter to undo me?
Dispel my doubts! My mind's awhirl;
Perhaps mere folly has created
These fancies of a simple girl
And quite another end is fated. . . .
So be it! Now my destiny
Lies in your hands, for you to fashion;
Forgive the tears you wring from me,
I throw myself on your compassion. . . .
Imagine: here I am alone,
With none to understand or cherish
*My restless thoughts, and I must perish,
Stifled, in solitude, unknown.
I wait: when once your look has spoken,
My heart once more with hope will glow,
Or a deserved reproach will show
The painful dream forever broken!

Reread I cannot. . . . I must end. . . .
The fear, the shame, are past endurance. . . .
Upon your honor I depend,
And lean upon it with assurance. . . .

[*1824*]

THE TALE OF THE GOLDEN COCKEREL [*]

In a realm that shall be nameless,
In a country bright and blameless,
Lived the mighty Czar Dadon,
Second in renown to none.
In his youth he would belabor
Without scruple every neighbor.
But he fancied, as he aged,
That enough wars had been waged—
Having earned a rest, he took it.
But his neighbors would not brook it,
And they harassed the old czar,
And they ruthlessly attacked him,
And they harried and they hacked him.
Therefore, lest his realm be lost,
He maintained a mighty host.
Though his captains were not napping,
They not seldom took a rapping:
In the south they're fortified—
From the east their foemen ride;
Mend the breach, as is commanded—
On the shore an army's landed
That has come from oversea.
Czar Dadon, so vexed was he,
Was upon the point of weeping,
Didn't find it easy sleeping.
Never was life bitterer!
So to the astrologer,
To the wise old eunuch, pleading
For his help, an envoy's speeding.
To the eunuch he bows low,
And the mage consents to go
At Dadon's behest, appearing

[*] The libretto of Rimsky-Korsakov's opera, Le Coq d'Or, is based on this tale.

70

At the court: a sign most cheering.
In his bag, as it befell,
He'd a golden cockerel.
"Set this bird," the mage directed,
"On a pole that's soon erected;
And my golden cockerel
Will protect thee very well.
When there is no sign of riot,
He will sit serene and quiet,
But if ever there should be
Threat of a calamity,
Should there come from any quarter
Raiders out for loot and slaughter,
Then my golden cockerel
Will arouse: his comb will swell,
He will crow, and up and doing,
Turn to where the danger's brewing."
In return the mage is told
He shall have a heap of gold,
And good Czar Dadon instanter
Promises the kind enchanter:
"Once thy wish to me is known,
'Twill be granted as my own."

On his perch, by the czar's orders,
Sits the cock and guards the borders—
And whenever danger's near
As from sleep our chanticleer
Rises, crows and fluffs his feathers,
Turns to where the trouble gathers,
Sounds his warning clear and true,
Crying: "Cock-a-doodle-doo!
Slug-a-bed, lie still and slumber,
Reign with never care or cumber!"
And the neighbors dared not seek
Any quarrel, but grew meek:

71

Czar Dadon there was no trapping,
For they could not catch him napping.

Peacefully two years go by,
And the cock sits quietly.
But one day, by noises shaken,
Czar Dadon is forced to waken.
Cries a captain: "Czar and Sire,
Rise, thy children's need is dire!
Trouble comes, thy realm to shatter."
"Gentlemen, what is the matter?"
Yawns Dadon. "What do you say?
Who is there? What trouble, pray?"
Says the captain: "Fear is growing,
For the cockerel is crowing:
The whole city's terrified."
The czar looked out and spied
The gold cockerel a-working—
Toward the east he kept on jerking.
"Quickly now! Make no delay!
Take to horse, men, and away!"
Toward the east the army's speeding
That the czar's first-born is leading.
Now the cockerel is still,
And the czar may sleep his fill.

Eight full days go by like magic,
But no news comes, glad or tragic:
Did they fight or not? Dadon
Has no message from his son.
Hark! Again the cock is crowing—
A new army must be going
Forth to battle; Czar Dadon
This time sends his younger son
To the rescue of his brother.
And this time, as at the other,

The brave cockerel grows still.
Now no news comes, good or ill.
And again eight days go flying,
And in fear the folk are sighing;
And once more the cockerel crows,
And a third host eastward goes.
Czar Dadon himself is leading,
Not quite certain of succeeding.

They march on, by day, by night,
And they soon are weary, quite.
Czar Dadon, in some vexation,
Vainly seeks an indication
Of a fight: a battleground,
Or a camp, or funeral mound.
Strange! But as the eighth day's ending,
We find Czar Dadon ascending
Hilly pathways, with his men—
What does his gaze light on then?
'Twixt two mountain peaks commanding,
Lo! a silken tent is standing.
Wondrous silence rules the scene,
And behold, in a ravine
Lies the slaughtered army! Chastened
By the sight, the old czar hastened
To the tent. . . . Alas, Dadon!
Younger son and elder son
Lie unhelmed, and either brother
Has his sword stuck in the other.
In the field, alackaday,
Masterless, their coursers stray
On the trampled grass and muddy,
On the silken grass now bloody. . . .
Czar Dadon howled fearfully:
"Children, children! Woe is me!
Both our falcons have been taken

In the nets! I am forsaken!"
All his army howled and moaned
Till the very valleys groaned—
From the shaken mountains darted
Echoes. Then the tent flaps parted . . .
Suddenly upon the scene
Stood the young Shamakhan queen!
Bright as dawn, with gentle greeting
She acknowledged this first meeting
With the czar, and old Dadon,
Like a night bird in the sun,
Stood stock still and kept on blinking
At the maid, no longer thinking
Of his sons, the dead and gone.
And she smiled at Czar Dadon—
Bowing, took his hand and led him
Straight into her tent, and fed **him**
Royally, and then her guest
Tenderly she laid to rest
On a downy couch, brocaded,
And by silken curtains shaded.
Seven days and seven nights
Czar Dadon knew these delights,
And, of every scruple ridden,
Did, bewitched, what he was bidden.

Long enough he had delayed—
To his army, to the maid,
Czar Dadon was now declaring
That they must be homeward faring.
Faster than Dadon there flies
Rumor, spreading truth and lies.
And the populace have straightway
Come to meet them at the gateway.
Now behind the coach they run,
Hail the queen and hail Dadon,

And most affable they find him . . .
Lo! there in the crowd behind him
Who should follow Czar Dadon,
Hair and beard white as a swan,
And a Moorish hat to top him,
But the mage? There's none to stop him;
Up he comes: "My greetings, Sire."
Says the czar: "What's thy desire?
Pray, come closer. What's thy mission?"
"Czar," responded the magician,
"We have our accounts to square;
Thou hast sworn, thou art aware,
For the help that I accorded,
Anything thy realm afforded
Thou wouldst grant me, my desire,
As thy own, fulfilling, Sire.
'Tis this maiden I am craving:
The Shamakhan queen." "Thou'rt raving!"
Shrieked Dadon forthwith, amazed,
While his eyes with anger blazed.
"Gracious! Hast thou lost thy senses?
Who'd have dreamed such consequences
From the words that once I said!"
Cried the czar. "What's in thy head?
Yes, I promised, but what of it?
There are limits, and I'll prove it.
What is any maid to thee?
How dare thou thus speak to me?
Other favors I am able
To bestow: take from my stable
My best horse, or, better far,
Henceforth rank as a boyar;
Gold I'll give thee willingly—
Half my czardom is for thee."
"Naught is offered worth desiring,"
Said the mage. "I am requiring

But one gift of thee. I mean,
Namely, the Shamakhan queen."
Then the czar, with anger spitting,
Cried: "The devil! 'Tis not fitting
That I listen to such stuff.
Thou'lt have nothing. That's enough!
To thy cost thou hast been sinning—
Reckoned wrong from the beginning.
Now be off while thou'rt yet whole!
Take him out, God bless my soul!"
The enchanter, ere they caught him,
Would have argued, but bethought him
That with certain mighty folk
Quarreling is not a joke,
And there was no word in answer
From the white-haired necromancer.
With his sceptre the czar straight
Rapped the eunuch on his pate;
He fell forward: life departed.
Forthwith the whole city started
Quaking—but the maiden, ah!
Hee-hee-hee! and Ha-ha-ha!
Feared no sin and was not queasy.
Czar Dadon, though quite uneasy,
Gave the queen a tender smile
And rode forward in fine style.
Suddenly there was a tinkling
Little noise, and in a twinkling,
While all stood and stared anew,
From his perch the cockerel flew
To the royal coach, and lighted
On the pate of the affrighted
Czar Dadon, and there, elate,
Flapped his wings, and pecked the pate,
And soared off . . . and as he flitted,
Czar Dadon his carriage quitted:

Down he fell, and groaned at most
Once, and then gave up the ghost.
And the queen no more was seen there:
'Twas as though she'd never been there—
Fairy tales, though far from true,
Teach good lads a thing or two.

[*1834*]

Yevgeny Boratynsky

THE ROAD OF LIFE

When Fate equips her sons, us fools, to take
The road of life, she would be kind, it seems,
For to each one she gives what is his due
In golden dreams.

The years post swiftly by and as they go
New stations beckon, greet us and are lost;
And with those golden dreams we duly pay
The journey's cost.

[1825]

"BLESSED ARE THEY"

Blessèd are they that righteousness proclaim!
But he who traces with discerning art
Some wicked convolution of the heart
Is not engulfed in the foul depths of shame.
Two regions—one of splendor, one of night—
We seek with equal zeal to scan aright.
An apple tumbles earthward from the tree,
And man perceives the law of heaven therein!
So sometimes in the merest hint we see
Revealed the dark significance of sin.

[1839]

"OF WHAT USE ARE YOU, DAYS?"

Of what use are you, days? There can be nothing
New for the mind to greet;
The world is full of things and all familiar,
And time can but repeat.

Not vainly did you strive in your impatience,
O frantic soul, to gain
Your full development before the body,
Which cannot slip its chain.

Since you have long since locked the sorry circle
Of sights beneath the moon,
You drowse, fanned by recurrent dreams; the body,
Accorded no such boon,

Must stupidly watch dawn arrive, relieving
The night for naught, and mark
A barren dusk, crown of a day that's empty,
Drop down into the dark.

[1840]

"PHYLLIDA"

Phyllida, as the nights grow colder,
With every winter that she sees,
Bares further her appalling shoulder,
A skeleton that strives to please;

And, a sepulchral Venus, brightly
Approaches the last couch of all,
As though before she slept she lightly
Let, one by one, her garments fall.

[1840]

PRAYER

King of Heaven, make me whole:
Grant Thy peace to my sick soul!
Let me know oblivion, Thou,
Of earth's error and earth's sin,
And with strength my heart endow
Thy stern paradise to win.

[1844]

Fyodor Tyutchev

AUTUMN EVENING

The light of autumn evenings falls serene,
All things in tender mystery arraying . . .
The trees in motley with their eerie sheen,
The languid airs through crimson leafage straying;
The tranquil azure that hangs dim and far
Above the earth wan with an orphan's sorrow,
And sometimes chilly gusts of wind that are
The harsh forerunners of a stormy morrow;
A withering, a waning, over all
A wistful smile that yields while it beseeches:
The look that in a rational soul we call
The sublime shyness only suffering teaches.

[1830]

"AS OCEAN HOLDS THE GLOBE"

As ocean holds the globe in its embrace,
So dreams about our earthly life are sweeping;
Night comes, and the sonorous billows chase
Each other, on the coast of darkness leaping.

That voice of dream, how urgently it sounds!
Alert, the magic skiff prepares to wander;
The tide swells swiftly, now the white sail rounds,
And we are borne to shoreless waters yonder.

Lo, the high heavens, starred and luminous,
Mysteriously from the deeps are gazing,
And we sail onward, while surrounding us
On every side the strange abyss is blazing.

1830

SILENTIUM

Be silent, secret, and conceal
Whate'er you think, whate'er you feel.
Within your soul your dreams should rise
And set like stars that fill the skies
With splendor on their nightly route:
Admire them, scan them, and be mute.

How can a heart at will unfold
Its tale? Can any soul be told
By what it is you live and die?
A thought when spoken is a lie.
The springs men dig for they pollute:
Drink secret waters and be mute.

Within yourself learn how to live.
Magic that is not fugitive
Lies, a rich treasure, in the mind,
Thoughts that the glare of day will blind
And the wild din without confute:
Heed that low music, and be mute.

1833

"THE SERVICE OF THE LUTHERANS"

The service of the Lutherans attracts me,
Their rite is simple, solemn, and austere,
These naked walls, this empty tabernacle
I like; I find their lofty lesson clear.

But look you: Faith, all ready for the journey,
For the last time is in your presence there;
True, she has not yet stepped across the threshold,
But her house stands already stripped and bare.

True, she has not yet stepped across the threshold,
Nor shut behind her the relentless door,
Ah, but the hour has struck. . . . Pray to the Lord, then:
For you will not be praying any more.

[1834] *1879*

TWILIGHT

Dove-colored, the shadows melt and mingle,
Color fades and sound has gone to sleep;
Motion is dissolved in distant rumours,
Undulant the dark, with life at neap. . . .
Beating the nocturnal air, a night moth
Is in flight, softly, invisibly. . . .
Hour of unutterable longing!
I am in the all, the all in me.

Gentle twilight, slumber-lidded twilight,
Brim my being with your quietness,
Let your silent, tender, fragrant languor
Rise in flood to tranquillize and bless.
Give my senses over to the darkness
Of pure self-forgetfulness to keep.
Let me taste annihilation, mix me
With the universe that lies asleep.

[1831–1836] *1879*

"WHY DO YOU HOWL SO MADLY, WIND OF NIGHT?"

Why do you howl so madly, wind of night?
What rage or grief is in your wordless cry?
What do you mean, strange voice that gives itself
To thunderous groans, then to a plaintive sigh?
In language long familiar to the heart

You speak of pain that none can comprehend,
Again and yet again; you moan, and now
Burst forth in savage sounds that pierce and rend.

Oh, hush those fearful songs whose music tells
Of primal chaos, our true element!
The secret world of the nocturnal soul
Harks to that tale, how breathlessly intent!
That soul would issue from the mortal breast,
Craving to join the infinite . . . Ah, no!
Do not arouse the storms that lie asleep.
Primeval chaos is astir below.

1836

"TEARS"

Tears, human tears, that pour forth beyond telling,
Early and late, in the dark, out of sight,
While the world goes on its way all unwittingly;
Numberless, stintless, you fall unremittingly,
Pouring like rain, the long rain that is welling
Endlessly, late in the autumn at night.

1850

JULY 14, AT NIGHT

Still the heat of mid-July
Lay upon night's glimmering air,
And above dim earth the sky
Shivered, as the storm drew nigh,
With heat lightnings' fitful flare.

Heavy lashes, so it seemed,
Parted, and the eyes they fringed,

When the swift heat lightnings gleamed,
On the earth abruptly beamed
With a look so fierce it singed.

1852

LAST LOVE

How tenderly, how superstitiously
We love when time has told its story. . . .
Shine, shine, departing light, and be
Crowned, late last love, with sunset's glory!

Long shadows cover half the sky,
Alone the west warm splendor casting;
Delay, delay, dusk, our good-by,
Enchantment, oh, be everlasting!

Let blood run thinner in the vein,
Heart's tenderness is not abated. . . .
Last love, you are the pitch of pain,
Of rapture and despair created.

1854

"OH, WIZARD SOUL"

Oh, wizard soul, oh, heart astir
And aching with your heavy trouble,
Upon the threshold of this double
Being, you waver, as it were.

And so two alien worlds you plumb:
Your day of morbid, passionate living,
Your sleep, vague revelations giving
Of heavenly visions yet to come.

Then let the tortured bosom beat
With fatal passion, mad vagary;
The soul is ready, even as Mary,
To cling forever to Christ's feet.

[1855]

"SORRY HAMLETS"

Sorry hamlets, niggard Nature,
Land that, patient, bears its yoke—
These are mine, this is my country,
Land of my own Russian folk!

Haughty foreign eyes can never
See your glory, never guess
The pure light that glimmers shyly
Through your humble nakedness.

Like a slave the King of Heaven
Tramped your roads on every hand;
Burdened with His cross He blessed you
Everywhere, my native land.

[1855]

"I KNEW HER"

I knew her in those fabled years
When, so it seems, the morning nears
And, as the hint of its first rays
Upon the azuring sky appears,
There sinks the star of primal days.

And in those sparkling early hours
The freshness wherewith nature dowers

The dark in which the morning stirs
And dew falls softly on the flowers,
Unheard, unseen—that charm was hers.

Her life was then a perfect thing,
A whole that asked no ripening,
From all our earthly fret so far,
I see it as not perishing
But only setting—like a star.

[1861]

"NOT WITH THE MIND"

Not with the mind is Russia comprehended,
The common yardstick will deceive
In gauging her: so singular her nature—
In Russia you must just believe.

[1866]

Alexey Koltzov

AN OLD MAN'S SONG

I shall saddle a horse,
A swift courser, he,
I shall fly, I shall race,
Lighter than a hawk,
Over fields, over seas,
To a distant land.
I shall overtake there
My first youth again.
I shall spruce myself up,
Be a blade again,
I shall make a fine show
For the girls again.
But alas! no road leads
To the bygone years,
And the sun will not rise
Ever in the west.

[*1835*]

Mikhail Lermontov

THE ANGEL

An angel was winging his way through the night,
   And softly he sang on his flight.
The moon and the stars and the clouds crowded near,
   That marvelous music to hear.

He sang of the bliss that is known by the blest
   Where the shadows of Paradise rest;
He sang of the greatness of God as he flew,
   His praise ringing holy and true.

He bore a young soul in his arms that must know
   The tears of the world and its woe.
Yet deep in that soul there lived, wordless and strong,
   The heavenly sound of his song.

Long years in the world did but sadden and tire
   One haunted by wondrous desire,
And dull earthly songs could not ever supplant
   For her that celestial chant.

[1831]

A SAIL

A far sail shimmers, white and lonely,
Through the blue haze above the foam.
What does it seek in foreign harbors?
What has it left behind at home?

The billows romp, and the wind whistles.
The rigging swings, the tall mast creaks.

It is not happiness he flees from,
Alas, it is not joy he seeks!

Below, the sea, like blue light flowing,
Above, the sun shines without cease,
But it is storm the rebel asks for,
As though in storm were peace.

[1832]

"SEE HOW HE GALLOPS" *

See how he gallops, with what dash and daring:
White hair is sometimes a delusive sign;
Thus an old, cobwebbed, mold-encrusted bottle
May hold a ready stream of sparkling wine.

[1836]

* These lines were written under the portrait of an elderly officer of the
hussars, a colleague of the poet's.

THE POET'S DEATH *

Now is the poet dead. Let honor claim
Her votary, though slander smirched his name.
Hot for revenge he met the unworthy foe;
Now is the proud heart pierced, the proud head low.
Too long a poet's soul endured the sting
Of shameful rumor and vain gossiping.
The false conventions of society
Roused him alone, and roused him but to die.
Slain! How shall sorrow speak now he is slain,

* The poet in question is Pushkin. The czar received anonymously a
MS. copy of the lament with the inscription: "A call to revolution."
Lermontov was arrested and, as a punishment, transferred from his hus-
sar regiment to a regiment of dragoons stationed in the Caucasus. The
translation is somewhat abridged.

When shouts of praise and sobs alike are vain?
Perhaps it was his destiny that willed;
But you, through whom her edict was fulfilled,
Who persecuted him, who kindled flame
Of genius merely to betray his name,
Your foul amusement is the epitaph
Of genius extinguished for a laugh.
The murderer's empty heart still sends the flow
Of cold blood through the hand that dealt the blow.
The pistol never trembled in that hand,
Nor could the sneering spirit understand
The tongue and customs of a foreign land.

Now he is dead, the prey of jealousy,
He and the songs he would have written die
To please the slanderers whose only joy
Is to deceive with gifts whom they destroy.
Their crown was laurel, but too clearly now
We see the hidden thorns that tore his brow.
Deceived and unavenged he lies at rest,
His songs in silence sleeping in his breast.

And you, degenerate descendants bred
In living evil from the evil dead,
Beslaverers of fortune, hearts of stone,
Greedy servility about the throne;
Hangmen of genius, liberty and fame,
Who hide behind the law's corrupted name—
The court and justice may condone your crime
But God's tribunal stands beyond all time.
The dread Judge waits, and on his lips, behold
No smile responds to clink of bribing gold.
Wash off the poet's righteous blood? In vain!
Your own eternal vileness spreads the stain.

[1837]

"WHEN THE YELLOW RYE–FIELD BILLOWS"

When the yellow rye-field billows in the breezes
And the fresh woods answer to the wind's low drum,
And deep in the orchard, hiding in the shadow
Of a cool green leaf, there hangs the purpling plum;

When, at rosy dusk or in the first gilt hours,
Sprinkled with fresh fallen, sweetly smelling dews,
From beneath the bushes, with a silver nodding
Lily of the valley greets me with her news;

When a cold brook ripples romping through the valley
And my thoughts are plunged, as its saga flows,
Into dim imaginings of the peaceful country
Whereof it is singing, land where it arose—

Then repose is granted to my troubled spirit,
Then no more with wrinkled brow I mope and plod,
And I can conceive of happiness on earth here,
And I can believe that in heaven I see God.

[1837]

CAPTIVE KNIGHT

Silent I sit by the prison's high window,
Where through the bars the untamed blue is breaking.
Flecks in the azure, the free birds are playing;
Watching them fly there, my shamed heart is aching.

But on my sinful lips never a prayer,
Never a song in the praise of my charmer;
All I recall are far fights and old battles,
My heavy sword and my old iron armor.

Now in stone armor I hopelessly languish,
And a stone helmet my hot head encases,

This shield is proof against arrows and swordplay,
And with no tug at the rein, my horse races.

Time is my horse, the swift-galloping charger,
I've for a visor this bleak prison grating,
My prison walls are my heavy stone armor;
Shielded by cast-iron doors, I am waiting.

Hurry, oh fast-flying Time, go more quickly!
In my new armor I suffocate, reeling.
I shall alight, with Death holding my stirrup,
And raise this visor, my cold face revealing.

[1840]

GRATITUDE

My thanks for all Thou gavest through the years:
For passion's secret torments without end,
The poisoned kiss, the bitterness of tears,
The vengeful enemy, the slanderous friend,
The spirit's ardor in the desert spent,
Every deception, every wounding wrong;
My thanks for each dark gift that Thou hast sent;
But heed Thou that I need not thank Thee long.

[1840]

"LAND OF MASTERS" °

Land of masters, land of slaves, farewell,
Unwashed Russia, it's good-by I say:
You in your blue uniforms, and you
Who were fashioned only to obey.

° Probably written when the poet was for the second time transferred
to the Caucasus. Some MS. copies have "czars" instead of "pashas" in
line 5.

From your pashas I may hide at last
Once the Caucasus between us rears,
And be safe from those all-seeing eyes
And unheard by those all-hearing ears.

[*1840*] *1887*

TESTAMENT

I'd like to be alone with you,
Brother, of course you won't say no:
The hours left me now are few;
I know it, they have told me so.

You'll soon be going home again,
So listen to me. . . . Oh, but then,
There's no one, to speak honestly,
Who cares much what becomes of me.

If someone asks . . . no matter who,
Just how it was that I went west,
Say I was wounded in the chest,
A bullet got me: I was through.

And tell them that I served the czar,
And honorably, understand;
Say, too, how poor our doctors are,
And that I greet my native land.

Father and mother won't be found,
I fear, by this time above ground,
And it is sorry I would be
Were grief to come to them through me.

So if you see one of them, say
That I am lazy with the pen,

And that we're in the field, and they
Should not expect me soon again.

They have a neighbor . . . time does fly,
It's long ago we said good-by,
And ask for me she never will,
I'm very sure of that . . . But still,

Tell her the truth and no white lie,
That empty heart you will not wring;
Just spill it, man, and let her cry—
Sure, tears to her don't mean a thing.

[1840]

MY COUNTRY

I love my country, but that love is odd:
My reason has no part in it at all!
Neither her glory, bought with blood,
Nor her proud strength hold me in thrall;
No venerable customs stir in me
The pleasant play of revery.
Ask me not why I love, but love I must
Her fields' cold silences,
Her somber forests swaying in a gust,
Her rivers at the flood like seas.
I love to rattle on rough roads at night,
My lodging still to find, while half awake
I peer through shadows left and right
And watch the lights of mournful hamlets quake.
I love the smoke above singed stubble rising;
I love a caravan that winds forlorn
Across the steppe; I love surprising
Two birches white above the yellow corn.
A well stocked barn, a hut with a thatched roof,

Carved shutters on a village window: these
Are simple things in truth,
But few can see them as my fond eye sees.
And on a holiday, from dewy dusk until
Midnight, it is a boon for me
To watch the dancers stomping to the shrill
Loud babble of the drunken peasantry.

[1841]

From THE DEMON: An Eastern Tale, XV

On the vast aerial ocean,
Through the mist how calmly steers
Star on star, to fill the heavens
With the music of the spheres.

Through the infinite blue meadows,
Through the boundless fields of space,
Clouds in shaggy flocks are straying,
Fugitives that leave no trace.

Hour of meeting, hour of parting,
Neither gladden them nor fret;
Theirs no yearning toward the future,
Theirs no haunting of regret.

On the dark day of misfortune
These remember, far away;
Be beyond earth's reach as they are,
And indifferent as they.

[1841] 1860

Nikolay Nekrasov

"ON PASSING THROUGH THE HAYMARKET"

On passing through the Haymarket last night
Somewhere near six o'clock, I chanced to see
A woman being whipped: a peasant girl
She was, who bore the lashes quietly.

No cry was forced from her, the only sound
Came from the whip that whistled through the air.
I called my Muse to me and bade her look:
"There is your sister—there!"

[1848]

"THE CAPITALS ARE ROCKED"

The capitals are rocked with thunder
Of orators in wordy feuds.
But in the depths of Russia, yonder
An age-old awful silence broods.
Alone the wind in wayside willows
Stirs with unceasing restlessness,
And in the endless fields the billows
Of arching stalks stoop to caress
The earth that cherishes and pillows.

[1857]

"MY VERSES!"

My verses! Living witnesses of tears
    For this forlorn earth shed!
Born in those moments when the storm wind rears

That fills the soul with dread,
Against the hearts of men you beat—who hears?—
   Like waves on cliffs as dead.

                              [*1858*]

FREEDOM *

Ah, Mother Russia, never yet have I
Traveled across your plains with heart so high!

I see a baby at its mother's breast
And by this stirring thought I am possessed:

Child, you were blest, in these times to be born;
Please God, it will not be your lot to mourn.

Free, and in dread of no man from the start,
You will yet choose the work after your heart;

You may remain a peasant all your years,
Or soar, with only eagles for your peers.

Perhaps my dream will cause a doubtful smile:
Man's mind is subtle and is full of guile;

Though serfdom's nets are broken, well I know
New snares have been contrived, as time will show;

But these the people will more readily
Break loose from: Muse, greet freedom hopefully.

                              [*1861*]

* *The emancipation of the serfs took place on February 19, 1861 (Old Style).*

NEWLYWEDS

So after the wedding, the husband
Must show off his goods to the bride:
"Look, woman, we've got a good cowshed,
But the cow—God would have it so—died!

"We've no featherbed and no bedstead,
But the bench here is warm, you can feel;
And though we've no calves, we've two kittens:
Just hark at them now, how they squeal!

"There are vegetables out in the garden:
Horseradish and onions I grew.
And if it is brassware you're wanting,
Here's a cross and a brass button, too."

[1866]

From WHO LIVES HAPPILY IN RUSSIA?

The Salt Song

There's nobody left but God. . . .
Maybe He knows the cure:
Not a mouthful my little one takes.
Ah, he will die for sure.

I gave him a bit of bread,
I gave him another bit.
He does not eat, he cries:
"Salt! Put salt on it!"

There is no salt in the house,
Never a pinch of it here.
"Try some flour," said God.
God whispered it in my ear.

The little one took a bite,
He made a face as he bit.
He cried, the tiny boy:
"Put more salt on it!"

I floured the crust again,
My tears rained on the bread.
The little one ate it up,
The little son was fed.

She boasted of her ruse:
She had saved him, it appears.
Ah, mother, mother,
Those were salty tears!

1876

Karolina Pavlova

"WE SHALL NOT OVERCOME OUR SORROWS"

We shall not overcome our sorrows
On earth by struggle proud and grim,
But only if to God we humble
Our hearts and lift our souls to Him,
Shall we, this earthly tribe of mortals,
Through grief and trouble safely flee,
As once of old the Jews passed over
The mounting, salty, evil sea!
And as the rising wall of waters
Supported them upon that day,
So shall our bitter, fateful sorrow
Be unto us a holy stay.

1862

Pyotr Vyazemsky

SPRING

"Ah, Spring, sweet Spring, chief pride of Nature!"
The air is foul, the ground is sludge;
Men curse the mud when they go walking,
And plunged in muck, a horse can't budge.

The cab breaks down, so does the carriage;
Season of colds in chest and nose,
To you, fair Spring, is reverence tendered
By cartwrights and by medicos.

1866

Alexey K. Tolstoy

"WHEN I AM PLAGUED"

When I am plagued with cares, amid life's noisy clamor,
Bruised by a thought that beats insistent as a hammer
Upon my mind, at times this blots your image out;
But when I am alone, and day, with all its doubt
And dread and vexing noise subsides, then too grows quiet
The turmoil of false life that in my soul held riot;
My mind becomes transparent as a placid lake
Whose very depths my plunging gaze can lightly rake;
Then clearly in my thoughts, unruffled and unmoved,
Your image is reflected, desired and beloved,
And I can see the bottom where, a dazzling prize,
My love for you in all its wealth and beauty lies.

1857

"SOLDIER OF NEITHER CAMP"

Soldier of neither camp, a casual guest in both,
I would rejoice to draw my sword in a just cause,
But secretly I chafe: both factions give me pause,
And neither can persuade these lips to take the oath.

My full allegiance, then, they cannot ever know—
My soul is still my own, though I choose either side:
The partial zeal of friends unable to abide,
I'd fight to keep unstained the banner of the foe.

[1858]

"A WELL"

A well, and the cherry trees swaying
Where bare girlish feet lately trod;
Near by a damp imprint betraying
A heavy nailed boot on the sod.

Hushed now is the place of their meeting,
But nothing the silence avails,
In my brain passion's echo repeating
Their whispers, the splash of the pails.

1858

"MY LITTLE ALMOND TREE"

My little almond tree
Is gay with gleaming bloom;
My heart unwillingly
Puts forth its buds of gloom.

The bloom will leave the tree,
The fruit, unbidden, grow;
And the green boughs will be
By bitter loads brought low.

1867

Apollon Maikov

"UPON THIS WILD HEADLAND"

Upon this wild headland, crowned meanly with indigent rushes
And covered with pitiful brush and the green of the pine trees,
The aged Meniskos, a fisherman, laid in his sorrow
His son who had perished. The sea had maternally nursed him,
That sea whose wide lap took him back, who resistlessly bore him
In death, and who carefully carried the young body shorewards.
Then mourning Meniskos went forth, and beneath a great willow
He dug him a grave, a plain stone he set for a mark on the cliffside,
And hung overhead a coarse net he had woven of willow—
A fisherman's wreath to be poverty's bitter memento.

[*1840*]

ART

Idly I cut me a reed by the shore where the sea heaves and thunders,
Dumb and forgotten it lay in my simple, my wind-beaten cabin.
Once an old traveler passed who remained for a night in our
dwelling
(Foreign his dress and his tongue, an old man who was strange to
our region).
Seeing the reed, he retrieved it, and cut the round ventages needful,
Lightly his lips he applied to the holes he had fashioned: responding
Swiftly, the reed was alive with the magical noise that would fill it
When at the edge of the sea, gentle Zephyros, ruffling the waters,
Touched the rough rushes to music and flooded the beach with the
sea-sound.

[*1841*]

SUMMER RAIN

"Golden rain! Golden rain! Out of the sky!"
Children sing out and run after the rain.
"Quiet, my children, we'll reap it again,
Only we'll gather the gold in the grain—
In the full granaries fragrant with rye."

[*1856*]

THE HAY HARVEST

The smell of hay is on the field,
  And singing as they go
The women toss the heavy yield
  And spread it row by row.

And yonder where the hay is dry
  Each man his forkful throws,
Until the wagon loaded high
  Is like a house that grows.

The poor old horse who draws the cart
  Stands rooted in the heat,
With sagging knees and ears apart,
  Asleep upon his feet.

But little Zhuchka speeds away
  In barking brave commotion,
To dip and flounder in the hay
  As in a grassy ocean.

THE SWELL *

Hushed is the storm, but the sea is like lead and it threatens.
Billows, like troops retiring from battle, are rushing,
Eagerly trying to outstrip each other, and bragging
One to another of trophies they've carried off with them:
Tatters of sky, pure blue,
Vanishing clouds' gold and silver,
Shreds of dawn's crimson.

[1887]

* From a cycle of poems entitled "Water Colors."

Yakov Polonsky

THE COSMIC FABRIC

This vast web, of Nature's weaving,
Is God's garment, so 'tis said.
In that fabric I—a living,
I—a still unbroken thread.
And the thread runs swiftly, never
Halting, yet if once it sever,
Seer or sage shall not suffice
The divided strands to splice.
For the Weaver so will veil it
That (let him who may bewail it)
None the ends shall ever find,
Nor the broken thread rebind.
Ceaselessly the threads are breaking—
Short, ah short will be my span!
Meanwhile at His fabric's making
Toils the cosmic artisan,
Curious patterns still designing,
Wave and crested hill defining,
Steppe and pasture, cloud and sky,
Wood and field of golden rye.
Vainly may the wise men scan it:
Flawless since that Hand began it,
Smooth and fine, with beauty stored,
Shines the garment of the Lord!

Afanasy Foeth

"A MAGIC LANDSCAPE"

A magic landscape,
My heart's delight:
A full moon's brightness,
A plain sheer white,

The high sky lighted,
The snow's pure ray,
And far-off gliding,
A lonely sleigh.

[*1842*]

"I COME AGAIN"

I come again with greetings new,
    To tell you day is well begun;
To say the leaves are fresh with dew
    And dappled in the early sun;

To tell you how the forest stirs
    In every branch of every brake,
And what an April thirst is hers,
    With every whistling bird awake;

To say, as yesterday, once more,
    With love as passionate and true,
My heart is ready as before
    For serving happiness and you;

To tell how over every thing
    Delight is blowing on the air—
I know not yet what I shall sing;
    I only know the song is there.

[*1843*]

"WHISPERS"

Whispers. Timid breathing. Trilling
Of a nightingale.
And below the runnel rocking,
Sleepy, silver-pale.

Strange nocturnal lights and shadows,
Shadows that enlace.
Row on row of magic changes
On the dearest face.

Smoky cloudlets, rose and purple,
With a tinge of fawn.
Kisses. Ah, and tears among them.
And the dawn, the dawn!

[*1850*]

AT THE FIRESIDE

The embers sink to ashes. In the dusk
A small transparent flame is wavering;
Thus on a scarlet poppy will a moth
Flutter an azure wing.

Drawn by a train of motley images,
The tired gaze is charmed, while all unclear,
Faces that alter as they flash and fade,
From the gray ashes peer.

The joy, the grief that were, arise once more,
Caressingly commingled, nor depart.
He lies who would deny the aching need
Of all that haunts the heart.

[*1856*]

ADDRESS TO DEATH

I know what fainting means, the heady sweetness
When the pain stops and dark comes in its stead;
And so quite fearlessly I can await you,
You night without a dawn, eternal bed.

Your hand may touch my head, and from life's records
You may expunge me, but I testify,
Before that hour, while yet my heart is beating,
Our powers are equal, and the victor: I.

A shadow at my feet, a faceless specter,
You, while I breathe, are subject unto me,
You are merely a thought that I am thinking,
The frail toy of my anguished revery.

[1884]

SWALLOWS

Calm Nature's idle spy, I follow
Her paths with pleasure; free and fond,
I watch the arrow-winged swift swallow
That curves above the dusking pond.

It swoops, its darting shadow smutching
The glassy surface, till one fears
Those perilous waters will be clutching
The sudden wing before it veers.

And once again the same quick daring,
And once again the same dark stream. . . .
Is not this flight our human faring?
Is not this urge our human dream?

110

Thus I, earth's creature, vainly chidden,
Seek out the alien way, and try
To enter the unknown, forbidden,
And scoop one drop of mystery.

[*1884*]

THE AERIAL CITY

At daybreak there spread through the heavens
Pale clouds like a turreted town;
The cupolas golden, fantastic,
White roofs and white walls shining down.

That citadel is my white city,
My city, familiar and dear,
Above the dark earth as it slumbers,
Upon the pink sky builded clear.

The distant aerial city
Sails northward, sails softly, sails high;
And there someone beckons, but offers
No pinions wherewith I might fly.

Vladimir Solovyov

"WITH WAVERING FEET I WALKED"

With wavering feet I walked where dawn-lit mists were lying,
To find the shores of wonder and of mystery.
Dawn struggled with the final stars, frail dreams were flying,
While unto unknown gods my morning lips were crying
The prayers that my dream-imprisoned soul had whispered me.

The noon is cold and candid, the road winds on severely,
And through an unknown land once more my journey lies.
The mist has lifted now, and the bare eye sees clearly
How hard the mountain road that rises upward sheerly,
How distant looms the dream the prescient heart descries.

Yet onward with unfaltering feet I shall be going
Till midnight, onward toward the shore of my desires,
Where, on a mountain height, new stars its glory showing,
My promised temple waits, with plinth and pillar glowing,
Beaten about with flames of white, triumphal fires.

1884

L'ONDA DAL MAR' DIVISA

The wave knows no contentment
When parted from the sea,
Whether it rises gently
Or rushes savagely;

It sighs ever and grumbles,
And whether bond or free,
It hungers for the boundless,
The fathomless blue sea.

[*1884*] *1891*

IMMORTALITY

Earth and water, air and stars,
All, except man's soul, 'tis sure,
Till the very end of time
Will continue, will endure.

Death is harmless to the dust
But can proudest dreams undo.
Envious, heart? Nay, be not so.
Soon we'll be immortal, too.

FORCE

She lies there, her full firm teats not denied
To ruinous Nero or meek Buddha, owing
The same to both who clutch her breasts, yes, knowing
The two as twins who suckle side by side.
She holds two vessels whence, forever flowing,
The streams of Life and Death serenely glide.
She breathes—and wreaths of stars are lit, and bide;
She breathes anew: they fly like sere leaves blowing.

She looks ahead with cold unseeing eyes;
Nor recks if she give life or cause to perish;
The children whom she nurtures she will cherish,
But when she weans them, every claim defies.
Evil and good gather them in thereafter
And play the cosmic game with idle laughter.

Dmitry Merezhkovsky

NIRVANA

As on the first day of Creation,
Blue heaven is serene again,
As though the world were free of anguish,
And the heart innocent of stain.

Not love, not fame are what I covet:
I breathe even as the grasses do
Here in the meadows' morning silence. . . .
I do not care to find a clue

To the lost past or count the coming
Days. All that I can feel is this:
What happiness not to be thinking,
Not to desire—what sheer bliss.

THE TRUMPET CALL

Underground there is a rustle
And a murmur and a bustle.
Trumpet voices fill the skies.
"Hark, they call us: brothers, rise!"
"No, the darkness holds, unshaken.
I would slumber, not to waken.
Do not rouse me. Do not call.
Do not strike the coffin wall."

"Sleep you cannot; do not flout us,
The last trump resounds about us.
They are rising from the tomb.
As from the maternal womb

Of the earth, the ancient mother,
Come the dead; 'tis your turn, brother!"

"No, I cannot come, nor will I.
I am dumb and blind, but still I
Know when I am proffered lies.
I will not, I will not rise!
Shame, brother, I've not forgotten:
I am dust now, foul and rotten!"

"God's will, brother, does not alter.
All shall rise, and none must falter.
All shall yet be judged by Him.
Cherubim and seraphim
High the holy throne are bearing.
Here our heavenly King is faring.
Brother, come, in any guise;
Glad or grieving, you shall rise."

PRAYER FOR WINGS

Prostrate, self-scorning,
Wingless and mourning,
Dust in the dust,
We lie as we must:
Empty. To dare not,
Know not and care not
Is our employ.
God, do Thou dower us,
Kindle, empower us,
Give us Thy joy.
Impotence clings—
How shall we bear it?
Wings, give us wings,
Wings of the spirit!

Fyodor Sologub

"IN A GAY JAR"

In a gay jar upon his shoulder
The slave morosely carries wine.
His road is rough with bog and boulder,
In the black sky no planets shine.
Into the dark with stabbing glances
He peers, his careful steps are slow,
Lest on his breast as he advances
The staining wine should overflow.

The ferment of a bitter foison
In a full amphora I bear:
There sleeps remembrance with its poison,
A brimming woe lies hidden there.
I follow secret ways and hidden
To guard the evil vessel, lest
A careless touch should pour unbidden
Its bitterness upon my breast.

"AUSTERE MY VERSE"

Austere my verse: therein are heard
Strange echoes, distant and despairing.
Are not my shoulders bowed in bearing
My inspiration's bitter word?

The dim day rests as shadows fall.
No road before me is unwinding:
My promised land I'll not be finding.
The world rears round me like a wall.

At times from that far land a vain
Faint voice resounds like distant thunder.
Can the long waiting on a wonder
Obliterate the long bleak pain?

"WE ARE WEARY"

We are weary of steering a course,
We are spent, it is rest that we crave,
      We are ripe
      For the grave.

Then as meek as the babe that is laid
In its cradle, there let us descend,
      To molder there soon,
         To no end.

"WHEN, TOSSED UPON THE
STORMY WATERS"

When, tossed upon the stormy waters,
I felt my ship was going down,
I cried aloud: "Oh, Father Satan,
Save me, nay, do not let me drown.

"Pray, let not my embittered spirit
Perish before its time: the price
Is all the sorry days before me
Pledged to the power of blackest vice."

The Devil seized me then and flung me
Into a leaky boat and frail;
Upon the bench two oars were lying,
And there I found an old gray sail.

Landward, into a life of evil,
I who was neither hale nor whole
Bore once again my sinful body
And my unclean, my outcast soul.

The vow I made you, Father Satan,
Made in an evil hour, I keep,
When I was sailing stormy waters
And you retrieved me from the deep.

And I will glorify you, Father,
No day from bitter blame exempt.
Above the world my curse shall tower,
And I will tempt—and I will tempt.

"EVIL DRAGON"

Evil dragon, in the zenith fiercely glowing,
Filaments of flame across the heavens throwing,
Thou whose fury scorches the deep vale each noon,
From my somber quiver I will pluck an arrow
Tipped with subtle poison that shall find thy marrow:
Evil dragon, thou exultest all too soon.

Boldly I will stand with my bow before thee,
Unawaited though foretold to triumph o'er thee;
Ruthless vengeance shall be mine to satisfy.
Brazen-voiced the arrow from the taut bow speeding,
Thou shalt answer with a heavy groan, and bleeding—
Evil slaughterer, thou shalt fade, sink, die.

THE DEVIL'S SWING

Beneath a shaggy pine,
Where the loud waters sing,

The hairy-handed fiend
Pushes his fiendish swing.

He shoves and gives a crow:
   To and fro
   To and fro.
The board creaks as it sags,
The rope is taut and drags
Against the heavy bough.

The weak, unsteady board
Creaks warningly and slides;
The devil can afford
To roar: he holds his sides.

In agony I swing:
   To and fro
   To and fro,
I swing and cling and try
To look away, but no,
He holds me with his eye.

Above the darkening pine
The blue fiend's tauntings ring:
"The swing has trapped you—fine!
Then, devil take you, swing!"

Beneath the shaggy pine
The demon voices sing:
"The swing has trapped you—fine!
Then, devil take you, swing!"

The fiend will not let go,
The dizzy board not stay
Until that dread hand falls
And I am swept away.

Until the hemp, rubbed thin
And frayed, breaks suddenly,
Until the broad black ground
Comes rushing up at me.

Above the pine I'll fling
And plop! into the mire.
Then swing, devil, swing—
Higher, higher, higher!

1907

Konstantin Balmont

"WITH MY FANCY I GRASPED"

With my fancy I grasped at the vague shadows straying,
At the vague shadows straying where the daylight had fled;
I ascended a tower, and the stairway was swaying,
And the stairway was swaying underneath my light tread.

Ever higher I climbed, ever clearer were rounded,
Ever clearer were rounded dreaming hilltops aglow;
And from heaven to earth twilight voices resounded,
Twilight voices resounded from above and below.

And the higher I rose, strange horizons defining,
Strange horizons defining, did the summits appear;
And my eyes as I gazed were caressed by their shining,
Were caressed by their shining, their farewell, sad and clear.

Now the night had appeared; earth in darkness lay dreaming,
Earth in darkness lay dreaming, like a slumbering star,
While the smoldering sun, his dim embers still gleaming,
His dim embers still gleaming, shone for me from afar.

I had learned to ensnare the vague shadows far straying,
The vague shadows far straying, where the daylight had fled:
Ever higher I rose, and the stairway was swaying,
And the stairway was swaying underneath my light tread.

1894

"LONG CENTURIES OF CENTURIES"

Long centuries of centuries will pass, unsighted
Millenniums as locusts in deathy clouds descend,

And to the muttering of centuries affrighted
The same enduring firmament will watch the end.
The dumb, dead firmament—that God will not remember,
Who breathes Eternity behind the farther skies,
Beyond the fading of the last star's last slow ember,
Beyond the utter threshold words may scrutinize.
Unto the bitter end, cold, alien, and appalling,
That starry desert will remain aloft in space,
When in a blaze of comets it will crumble, falling
Like tears that dumbly drop from a despairing face.

"THE PSALM OF SILENCE"

The Psalm of Silence rises, candid, chaste;
Burning with sunsets lies the icy waste;
The elements are lost in reveries,
Serene the voiceless polar liturgies.

The sea of whiteness wears a scarlet hood,
This crystal kingdom knows nor field nor wood;
Altars of ice look up toward heaven's calm,
A prayer not suppliant soars, a wordless Psalm.

1908

Valery Brusov

"RADIANT RANKS"

Radiant ranks of seraphim
Stir the air about our bed.
With their pinions cool and dim
Our hot cheeks are comforted.

Low the circling seraphs bend,
And we tremble and rejoice
At hosannas that ascend,
Winged with their unearthly voice.

Cloudy luminous faces hover,
And the wing-swept candles wane,
And our fiery breasts they cover
With a viewless holy rain.

[1905]

THE COMING HUNS

"Trample their Eden, Attila!"—VYACHESLAV IVANOV

Where do you wait, coming Huns,
Who weigh on the world like a cloud?
Under the Pamirs' suns
Your cast-iron tread is loud.

Swoop down in a drunken horde
From your dark tents on the plains,
Let a wave of blood be poured
Into these empty veins.

123

O slaves of freedom, raise
Your tents on the palace site;
Where once the throne would blaze,
Let your grainfields glow as bright.

Heap books to build a fire!
Dance in the merry light.
The holy place bemire:
You are children in our sight.

And we, the poets, the wise,
Shall be true to the treasures we save,
Hiding the torch you despise
In catacomb, desert, and cave.

Where angry lightnings glance,
Where tempests raven and tear,
What will the play of chance
From our long labors spare?

All that we alone knew
May be blotted out by your whim.
Yet you who destroy me, you—
I salute with hosanna and hymn.

[1905]

THE TRYST

In the land of Ra the flaming, by the shores of Nile's slow waters,
    where Lake Moeris spread its sheen,
In the days of yore you loved me, as dark Isis loved Osiris, sister,
    friend, and worshiped queen!
And the pyramid its shadow on our evening trysts would lean.

Oh, the mystery remember of our meeting in the temple, as the
    shadows seemed to blend

124

When, the candles all extinguished and the sacred dances broken,
   each to each was instant friend,
Our enchanted touch and whisper, leaping joy that could not end!

In the splendor of the ballroom, clinging to me, white and tender,
   through Time's curtain rent in twain,
Did your ear not catch the anthems, mingling with the crash of cym-
   bals, and the people's answering refrain?
From the sleep of separation we had waked, you vowed, again!

Once before we knew existence, this our bliss is a remembrance, and
   our love—a memory;
Casting off its ancient ashes, flames again our hungry passion, flames
   and kindles you and me—
As of old by Nile's slow waters in that hour of destiny.

[1906]

ST. SEBASTIAN

In slow and smoky fires thou burn'st and art consumèd,
   Oh, thou, my soul.
In slow and smoky fires thou burn'st and art consumèd—
   With wordless dole.

Thou standest like Sebastian, pierced with pointed arrows,
   Harassed and spent.
Thou standest like Sebastian, pierced with pointed arrows,
   His young breast rent.

Thy foes encircle thee and watch with gleeful laughter
   And bended bow.
Thy foes encircle thee and watch with gleeful laughter
   Thy torments slow.

The embers burn and gentle is the arrow's stinging
   As night descends.
The embers burn and gentle is the arrow's stinging:
   Thy trial ends.

Why hastens not thy dream unto thy lips, now pallid
   With deathy drouth?
Why hastens not thy dream unto thy lips, now pallid,
   To kiss thy mouth?

                                                    [1907]

INEVITABILITY

If you were true or not, what matter? Say
Mine was an idle habit of forsaking—
What matter? For we cannot look away.
The bond that holds us was not of our making.
Once more you pale, as once more I am shaking
With prescience of the pain we cannot stay.
The moments pour with noise of torrents streaming:
Above us passion's lifted blade is gleaming.

Call it or God or Fate that thus created
This thirst of each for each that naught can quell.
Within the magic circle, blessed or fated,
We stand, beyond escape now from the spell!
Bowed by our fear if by our joy elated,
We sink like anchors under the sea-swell.
Not chance, nor tenderness, nor love defeated
Us, whom the ineluctable has greeted.

                                                    [1908]

BENEDICTION

"Que tes mains soient bénies, car elles sont impures."
                                    —REMY DE GOURMONT

The shining of your golden eyes I bless!
It broke my dark delirium with light.

126

The smile that wavers on your lips I bless!
Like wine it held me with its subtle might.

The poison in your kisses hid I bless!
All thoughts, all dreams are poisoned by your kiss.

The scythe that sings in your embrace I bless!
All my past years you have mown down with this.

The kindling fire of your love I bless!
I wrapped its flame about me joyfully.

The darkness of your spirit, lo, I bless!
For that its wings were outstretched over me.

Blessed all you gave, blessed what your soul denies;
I bless you for the fears, the agonies,

That after you I strove toward paradise,
That here, without its gates, I stand and freeze!

[1908]

EVENTIDE

The posters shout, their glowing motley blares,
The signboards groan above the passers-by,
And from the shops a sharp light shrilly flares
And stings the sense like a triumphant cry.

Behind the glimmering panes soft fabrics sleep,
And diamonds pour out their poison daze;
Like northern lights the lottery numbers leap
Above heaped coins that form a star ablaze.

The burning streets like long canals of light
Flow on and on—the city is alive.
It celebrates the rising tide of night
Swarming with countless freaks like some huge hive.

The sky is dimmed, its sentient stars put out
Where steadily the blue-rayed arc lamps burn
Coldly for whores and sages, the whole rout
Of jostling dancers as they twist and turn.

Between the gay quadrilles that form and break,
Among the waltzing couples, clanking slide
The trolleys, with blue lightnings in their wake;
And motors fling their sheaves of fire wide.

Shame like a leader wields his bright baton
Above the raucous music of the wheels,
Fusing the thousand voices into one
That as a mighty sacred chorus peals:

"We celebrate thy majesty, O Dust,
And, thy exalted name to glorify,
Dance round electric altars where they thrust
Their javelins into an empty sky!"

[1909]

Georgy Chulkov

AUTUMNAL LOVE

Purple Autumn unloosed her tresses and flung them
On the heavens and over the dew-heavy fields.
She came as a guest to the old, silent manor,
Singeing the grasses with red;
Through the garden she sauntered,
Then she climbed up the balcony, barely
Touching the fragile old rails.
She pushed the door softly,
Softly she entered the room,
Sprinkling the rug with her yellowish sand,
Dropped a red leaf upon the piano. . . .

From that hour on, we heard her unceasing rustle,
Rustle and stir and soft whisper.

And our hands suddenly met
With no new words, new and forever false:
As though we had hung a wreath of red roses
On a black, wrought-iron door
Leading into a vault
Where rotted the dear remains
Of a beloved dream.

Autumnal days were upon us,
Days of inscrutable longing;
We were treading the stairs
Of autumnal passion.
In my heart a wound, like an icon lamp,
Burned and would not be quenched.
The cup of autumnal poison
We pressed to our lips.

By the serpentine garden path Autumn had led us
To the pond lilies,
To the pool edged with worn sands.
And over the lilied waters and in the roses of evening,
We loved, more superstitiously.

And through the dark night,
On the languorous bed,
At the feet of my love,
I loved death anew.
The minutes rang tinkling like crystals
At the brink of an autumn grave:
Autumn and Death drunkenly clinked their glasses.

I pressed my thirsty lips
To the feet the icon lamp ruddied,
I drank the cup of love.
Scorched by the fires of crimes,
Stretched on the cross of lusts,
Filled with shame at needless betrayals,
I drank the cup of love.

In the hour of ineffable dalliance
I sensed the whisper
Of autumnal, of deathbed passion.
And kisses like keen needles
Burned and pierced,
Weaving a wreath of thorns.

Viktor Hofman

SUMMER BALL

The evening of the ball was hushed,
The summer ball, with scarce a quiver
In the dark lindens where they brushed
The sharpest curve of that still river.

Where, on the river's very brink,
The willows drooped like drowsy dreamers,
There it seemed beautiful to link
The banners and the colored streamers.

A singing waltz that dreamed and sighed,
And many glances, meeting, swerving,
Soft clouds that, tenderly enskied,
Seemed women's shoulders, softly curving.

The river looked a sculptured stream,
Or else the heavens' still reflection,
Their miracle's exultant gleam
Revived in fading recollection.

The clouds were hemmed with broader gold
Where, faint, a crimson gleam was clinging.
Serene the dream that thus could hold
The waltz, still summoning and singing.

A waltz, with linden boughs above,
And many glances, meeting, swerving,
And near, ah, near, the wonder of
Someone's long lashes softly curving.

1905

Vasily Bashkin

EAGLES

Upon the black brow of a cliff where no life ever stirred
Alighted strong, hoary-winged eagles, grave bird upon bird.

They whetted their claws on the rock, sitting massive and glum,
And loudly they called on their lately-fledged comrades to come.

How sure was the beat of their great heavy wings on the skies;
A furious strength was ablaze in their obdurate eyes.

To each new arrival their welcome was savagely clear:
"Hail, comrade! Delay not! The days we have longed for are near!"

Mikhail Kuzmin

THIS SUMMER'S LOVE

4.

Night was done; we rose and after
Washing, dressing, kissed with laughter.
Past was all the sweet night knows.
Lilac breakfast cups were clinking
While we sat like mere friends drinking
Tea—and kept our dominoes.

And our dominoes smiled greeting,
And our eyes avoided meeting
With our dumb lips' secrecy.
Faust we sang, we played, defying
All night meant, its gifts denying,
As though night's twain were not we.

[*1906*]

From ALEXANDRIAN SONGS

I.

How I love the world in all its beauty,
O eternal gods!
The sun, how I love it, the reeds,
and the greenish glitter of the sea
through the slender acacia branches!
How I love books (those of my friends),
the hush of my lonely house,
and the view from the window
overlooking the melon patches!
How I love the bright crowds in the square,

the shouting voices, the singing, and the sun,
the lively laughter of boys playing ball,
the return home
after a pleasant stroll,
in the evening
when the first stars are out,
past the inns with windows already alight,
companioned by a friend who has become remote!
O eternal gods, how I delight
in serene melancholy,
in love that is brief,
in death that does not regret the passing of a life
whose every feature is cherished,
and which, I swear by Dionysos, I love
with all the strength of my heart
and of the flesh that is so dear to me!

II.

Dying is sweet
on the battlefield
in the hissing of arrows and spears,
when the trumpet sounds
and the sun of noon
is shining,
dying for country's glory
and hearing around you:
"Hero, farewell!"
Dying is sweet
for an old, venerable man
in the house
on the bed
where his forebears were born and died—
surrounded by children
grown men,
and hearing around him:
"Father, farewell!"

134

But sweeter,
wiser,
having spent the last obol,
having sold the last mill
for a woman
who the next day is forgotten,
having come
from a gay promenade
to the mansion already sold,
to sup
and, having read the tale of Apuleius
for the hundred and first time,
to open your veins
in the warm, fragrant bath,
hearing no farewell;
and through the high slit of a window
must come the scent of stock,
dawn must be glowing,
and flutes be heard in the distance.

1908

"NOW DRY YOUR EYES"

Now dry your eyes, and shed no tears:
In heaven's straw-pale meadows veers
Aquarius, and earthward peers,
His empty vessel overturning.
No gusty snows, no clouds that creep
Across the sheer pure emerald steep,
Whence, thinly drawn, a ray darts deep
As a keen lance with edges burning.

[1911]

Vyacheslav Ivanov

THE SEEKING OF SELF

Dying, the seed will discover the self it finds in the losing.
  That is, O Nature, thy law! That is thy gospel, O Man!

Hearing dark music, the poet knows no repose as he listens—
  Clearer and clearer the sound, purer the fore-uttered word.

1903

NARCISSUS: A POMPEIAN BRONZE

Beautiful boy, like a faun here in loneliness roaming, who art thou?
  Surely no child of the woods: thine is too noble a face.

Both the firm grace of thy gait and the sumptuousness of thy sandal
  Tell thou art son to the gods, or the high offspring of kings.

Listening, slowing thy pace, the unrevealed sound thou hast fol-
    lowed,
  Charmingly bending thy head, moving thy finger in time.

Was it the piping of Pan or the amorous sighing of Echo,
  Babble of naiads at play, reticent dryads' low speech?

Leaning a hand on thy thigh, like Liaeus thou twinest thy fingers
  Daintily in the light fleece that thy smooth shoulders support.

Wonderful, art thou not Bacchus himself, by Nysaean nymphs
    cherished?
Hunter whom goddesses loved, naked and idle and young?

Or art thou haughty Narcissus, alone with his reveries, roving
  Languidly, seeking to snare harmonies heard in his dream?

136

Go, seek the summoning nymph, O thou blind one, not knowing
   thy image,
   Go thou, but dare not to bend over the slumbering wave.

For, if thou art not Narcissus, then, seeing thy image reflected,
   Stranger, ah, sorely I fear, thou a Narcissus wilt be.

1904

NOMADS OF BEAUTY

"You are artists, nomads of Beauty."
—Torches

For you—ancestral acres,
And, choked, the graveyard waits.
For us, the free forsakers—
The prairies Beauty fates.

For us—the daily treason,
The camps we daily flee,
Who break with each new season
A false captivity.

Trust distance for its marvels,
All veils as sheer disguise,
The springtide's emerald carvels,
The breadth of all the skies.

Oh, vagrant artists, shepherd
Your droves of dreams unbound;
And sow, although you jeopard
The soon-abandoned ground.

And from your open spaces
Rush down, a whirling horde,

Where slaves tamed to the traces
Adore their overlord.

Destroy their Eden's bowers!
Where bare and virgin lies
The land, there your steppe flowers
And there your stars will rise.

1904

"THE HOLY ROSE"

The holy rose her leaves will soon unfold.
The tender bud of dawn already lies
Reddening on the wide, transparent skies.
Love's star is a white sail the still seas hold.
Here in the light-soaked space above the wold,
Through the descending dew the arches rise
Of the unseen cathedral, filled with cries
From the winged weavers threading it with gold.

Here on the hill the cypress, in accord
With me, stands praying, a cowled eremite.
And on the rose's cheeks the tears fall light.
My cell is festive where bright rays are poured.
And in the east the purple vines bleed bright
And seething overflow. . . . Hosanna, Lord!

VESPERS

III.

Clear the fountain waters glowing,
Living streams, the wellsprings flowing,
Cold, in darkling woods, a spring.
In the shed, cool stillness streaming,
O'er the well, a candle gleaming
On Christ's crown its gilding flings.

In the Eden field—a bower,
And a fountain, and a flower.
Christ, star-voiced, the spirit stills:
"Come, before my wellspring stooping,
Of my quiet waters scooping—
For the stintless bucket fills."

V.

Now the golden leafage is beggared.
Shining through the porches of autumn
Shows the cool, blue stillness of heaven.
Lo, the thin-trunked grove is transcended:
Carved in stone, a columned cathedral.
Smoke scrolls wind about the white pillars.

Hung above the portal are curtains—
Openwork: like nets of God's fishers
That the catch has slipped through and broken,
Like thy tatters, humble and sacred,
At the entrance to a white temple,
Oh, thou golden, mendicant music!

1908

FUNERAL

Of funerals, the saddest
Is love's that dies unanswered.
The soul has two to bury:
The soul of the beloved
And its own other selfhood.
And a third enters, living,
The funeral flame that wraps them;
His wings a yoke has weighted:
Him the wise lips of lovers
Call in their kisses Eros,
And gods, the Resurrector.

FALLOW LAND AND STUBBLE FIELDS

III.

Sadness and stillness. What a bright transparency!
Enskied a woman seems to stand invisibly
Holding a crystal balance and intently poring
Over the instant, its frail equipoise adoring.

But every yellow leaf that from the branches sails,
Laying its little weight of gold upon the scales,
May force the pan ripe summer's bounty freighted
Towards the grave whereto the world of light is fated.

1914

WINTER SONNETS

III.

The winter of the soul . . . the living sun
Warms it obliquely and from far away.
But the dumb drifts rise up to blind and stun
A spirit lulled by the lone blizzard's lay.
Come, place the firewood, and the hearth flame leaps
To cook your sup of porridge busily;
The hour suffices; then, with all that sleeps,
Sleep, too. Oh, deep grave of Eternity!

Ice-choked, life's wellspring lies beneath a cloud,
The fount of fire is no longer brave. . . .
Oh, do not seek me under my close shroud.
My double drags his coffin, a meek slave;
But I, the true self, flesh cannot command,
Toil at the temple builded by no hand.

1920

Andrey Belyi

"ONCE MORE I PRAY"

Once more I pray, as doubt torments me and appals;
The saints with a dry finger threaten from the walls.

Stern faces like black spots upon the icons show,
And, dark with centuries, the gilt has lost its glow.

But now the window is aflood with streaming rays,
And in the molten sun all is alive, ablaze.

"Thou gentle light," the choir is chanting, and behold,
The saints' dark faces gleam with a puce-colored gold.

And, incense-wreathed, the priest moves altarward as one
Who as a nimbus wears this ecstasy of sun.

1903

REQUIEM

I.

"You sit on the bed there
In the sunset's full crimson,
Pillows crumpled,
Looking distracted—what
Troubles you?"

> "Oh, swept by
> Transparent
> Gold cataracts,
> The fir-tree tops
> Loom athwart the sky's blue."

"Orphaned, alone, I shall
Languish
Through summer
Twilights and winter nights.
There are new flights, but
Try them I dare not.
Oh, do not die!"

> "Oh, above the pines
> I float off into ether seas.
> Who there, what there
> Swathes the sky with whitenesses
> As with vestments of silver?"

1907

FIELDS

It is a wolf's hunched back that bristles
And flashes there along the rise.
Upon the azured snow the shadow
With what light leaps in silence flies.

Now it is dropping down an incline,
Below a fir now shrinks away.
A dog cries in the wintry distance,
Getting the scent, and hugs the sleigh.

What power is theirs: the night, the mournful
Expanse, and panic fantasy,
This thunder-throated icy powder,
The heavens' austere finery.

1907

BRIGHT DEATH

The shining and ponderous goblet
I empty: the earth drops below me,

142

All things sink away—I am treading
Cold space—the vast void—the dim ether.
But constant, in ancient space looming,
My radiant goblet: the Sun.

I look—far below me are lying
The rivers, the forests, the valleys,
Estranged in the vanishing distance,
A cloud, blowing fog on my eyelids,
Trails gossamer gold in its going.

The flickering landscape is burning
Its last: midday stars newly kindled
Look into my soul, sparkling: "Welcome,"
With radiance silently streaming:
"The end of long wanderings, brother,
Lies here, in your motherland, welcome!"

Slow hour upon hour in procession,
Slow centuries, smiling, pass onward.
In ancient space proudly I lift it,
My radiant goblet: the Sun.

1909

CHRIST IS RISEN

22

And the news
Pealed:
A hosanna.

A strange
Flame
Is revealed
In the cave of unfaith.

143

And behold!
The murk,
Irradiate, owns
It is dawn,
And our bodies
Are rolled
Away from us—

Even as stones.

23

Russia,
My country—

Thou art
That Woman clothed with the sun
To whom
All eyes
Are lifted. . . .

I see clearly:

Russia,
My Russia,
Is the God-bearer
Overcoming
The Serpent. . . .

The peoples
Inhabiting Thee
Have stretched out
Their hands
Through the smoke

To Thy spaces
That are filled with song,
Filled with the fire
Of a descending seraph.

And my throat
Locks with emotion.

24

I know:
An airy vast
Is shed
Round each of us
Like a nimbus;

Each man's head
Glows
With lightnings raying from
This age's
Embered woes.

And the Word that now
Stands midmost of the heart,
Of the storm-trumpeted
Spring,
Swelling the voiceful depths
Of its fiery throat,
Breaks prison:

Dearly beloved
Sons—
Christ is Risen.

1918

Alexander Blok

"I HAVE FOREKNOWN THEE"

*"Longing and loving, you shall yet slough off
The heavy sleep of earthly consciousness."*
—Vladimir Solovyov

I have foreknown Thee! Oh, I have foreknown Thee. Going,
The years have shown me Thy unalterable face.

Intolerably clear, the farthest sky is glowing.
I wait in silence Thy longed-for and worshiped grace.

The farthest sky is glowing: soon Thou wilt be nearing.
Yet terror clings to me: Thy image will be strange,

And insolent suspicion will rouse at Thy appearing;
The features long foreknown, beheld at last, will change.

How shall I then be fallen, undone by the surrender
Unto my deathy dream, bowing to bitter change!

The farthest sky is glowing; nearer looms the splendor!
Yet terror clings to me: Thy image will be strange.

[*1901*]

"A LITTLE BLACK MAN"

A little black man ran through the town.
He extinguished the street lamps, high on his ladder.

Dawn was approaching, white and slow.
With the strange little man it climbed the ladder.

Where soft, silent shadows, black and brown,
Where the lamplight's yellow stripes had been sleeping,

Morning twilight upon the steps lay down,
Into the curtains, into the door cracks creeping.

Ah, how pale is the city when night has died!
The little black man is crying now, outside.

[1903]

LITTLE CATKINS *

Little boys and little maidens
Little candles, little catkins
   Homeward bring.

Little lights are burning softly,
People cross themselves in passing—
   Scent of spring.

Little wind so bold and merry,
Little raindrops, don't extinguish
   These flames, pray!

I will rise tomorrow early,
Rise to greet you, Willow Sunday,
   Holy day.

1906

* On the eve of Palm Sunday, which the Russians call Willow Sunday, consecrated sprigs of pussy willow and lighted candles are carried home from church.

THE STRANGER

Of evenings now above the restaurants
Heavily hangs the thick and troubled air;

The spirit of spring, brooding, pestilent,
Governs the drunken outcries rising there.

Beyond the dusty alleys and beyond
The boredom of the summer villas gleams
The faint gold sign over the bakery,
And in the distance sound the children's screams.

This is the hour when the practiced wags,
Their derbies cocked, pass out beyond the town
To meet the ladies by the sad canals
And to parade there slowly up and down.

Thinly upon the lake the oarlocks creak,
The women shriek, and in its usual place
Up in the heavens the indifferent moon,
Bored with it all, pulls a stupid face.

Reflected every evening in my glass,
The sole companion of my solitude,
I see one friend, by the strange acrid wine,
Even as I, befuddled and subdued.

And at the neighboring tables, wearily
The drowsy waiters watch the hours pass
As pass they must, while drunks with rabbits' eyes,
Blinking, cry out: *"In vino veritas!"*

And every evening at the appointed hour
(Or is it but a dream I dream again?)
The figure of a girl in shining silks
Is seen to move across the foggy pane.

She slowly picks her way among the drunks,
And always uncompanioned, all alone,
Breathing of fragrance as of mist, she comes
To sit beside the window, the unknown.

148

From her resilient silks and mournful plumes
And from her narrow hands with their great rings
Legends are wafted: the air round her stirs
With wordless whispers of mysterious things.

By her strange nearness held as by a spell,
I peer behind her somber veil and see
The fairy gleam of an enchanted shore,
And an enchanted vista beckons me.

I am made master of unspoken things,
Another's sun is given me to keep,
Into the secret places of my soul
The acrid wine has found a way to creep.

And in my brain the ostrich feathers toss
Their plumy curves and sink and sway and rise,
And on the distant shore mysteriously
Flower two wide and fathomless blue eyes.

Deep in my soul a secret treasure lies,
The key thereto is mine and only mine!
Yes, drunken monster, you made no mistake!
I know, I know: truth lies in wine.

[*1906*]

"I PLANTED MY BRIGHT PARADISE"

To My Mother

I planted my bright Paradise
And hid it with a paling tall;
Through azure air for her dear son
I heard my mother cry and call:

149

"Dear son, where are you?" No reply,
The light above my palisade
Is slowly turning richly ripe
The secret vineyard I have made.

With care my mother treads around
My fenced and fruitful garden bowers,
And calls again: "Where are you, son?"
So careful not to crush the flowers.

And all is quiet. Does she know
A hidden heart grows ripe and wise,
And he is done with other joys
Who tastes the wine of Paradise?

1907

"WHEN MOUNTAIN ASH
IN CLUSTERS REDDENS"

When mountain ash in clusters reddens,
Its leafage wet and stained with rust,
When through my palm the nail that deadens
By bony hands is shrewdly thrust,

When o'er the rippling, leaden river,
Nailed to the cross, in agony,
Upon the wet gray height I quiver,
While, stern, my country watches me,

Then far and wide in anguish staring
My eyes, grown stiff with tears, will see
Down the broad river slowly faring,
Christ in a skiff approaching me.

And in his eyes the same hopes biding,
And the same rags from Him will trail,

His garment piteously hiding
The palm pierced by the final nail.

Christ! saddened are the native reaches.
The cross tugs at my failing might.
Thy skiff—will it achieve these beaches,
And land here at my cruciate height?

1907

"SHE CAME OUT OF THE FROST"

She came out of the frost,
Her cheeks glowing,
And filled the room with
Freshness of air and perfume,
A ringing voice
And chatter
Utterly disrespectful
Of serious pursuits.

She proceeded to drop
A fat volume of an art review
On the floor,
And suddenly
My room
Began to look fearfully crowded.

All this was somewhat annoying
And rather absurd.
She asked me, however,
To read *Macbeth* to her.
When I came to: "The earth hath bubbles . . ."
(I cannot say it without agitation),
I noticed she too was agitated
And was staring out of the window.

It appears that a large spotted tomcat
Was cautiously crawling
Along the edge of the roof
After two doves that were billing.

I got angry, chiefly
Because the doves, not we, were kissing,
And the days of Paolo and Francesca were gone.

1908

"HOW NARROW IS THE CIRCLE"

How narrow is the circle of our being:
As all roads lead to Rome, we can foresee
The past stretching ahead into a future
That will repeat the pattern slavishly.

I, like all others, know what lot awaits me
As I proceed upon my darkening way:
Again to love Her where She reigns in heaven
Whom here on earth I shall again betray.

1909

"YES. THUS HIS DAEMON"

Yes. Thus his Daemon to the poet speaks:
My freeborn fantasy returns again
To cling to darkness and to poverty
Where the insulted dwell in filth and pain.
Down, down, go plumb the meekest misery,
The other world is more distinct from there.
Have you seen children on the Paris streets,
Or beggars on the bridge in wintry air?
Open your eyes, be quick to open them

To life's absolute horror, see it clear
Before your land is swept by the great storm
That will lay waste whatever tenants here.
Let righteous anger ripen, let it swell;
Prepare your hands for toil: you dare not turn
Away. . . . If you are helpless, let your rage
And your despair grow in your breast and burn.
Do this at least: wipe from a life of lies
The oily rouge that suits its face so ill;
Go play the frightened mole and dig yourself
A place far underground and there be still,
Alone, morose, bitterly hating life,
Despising this black world and all its ways,
And if not glimpsing what the future holds,
Stern in denial of these present days.

[*1911–1914*]

"TO SIN, UNSHAMED"

To sin, unshamed, to lose, unthinking,
The count of careless nights and days,
And then, while the head aches with drinking,
Steal to God's house, with eyes that glaze;

Thrice to bow down to earth, and seven
Times cross oneself, and then once more
With the hot brow, in hope of heaven,
To touch the spittle-covered floor;

With a brass penny's gift dismissing
The offering, the holy Name
To mutter with loose lips, in kissing
The ancient, kiss-worn icon frame;

153

And to come home, then, and be tricking
Some wretch out of the same small coin,
And with a hiccough to be kicking
A trembling cur in his lean groin;

And where the icon's flame is quaking
Drink tea, and reckon loss and gain,
From the fat chest of drawers taking
The coupons marked with spittle stain;

And sunk in feather beds to smother
In slumber such as bears may know—
Dearer to me than every other
Are you, my Russia, even so.

1914

THE HAWK

Over the empty fields a black hawk hovers,
    And circle after circle smoothly weaves.
In the poor hut, over her son in the cradle,
    A mother grieves:
"There, suck my breast: there, grow and eat our bread,
And learn to bear your cross and bow your head."

Time passes. War returns. Rebellion rages.
    The farms and villages go up in flame,
And Russia in her ancient tear-stained beauty,
    Is yet the same,
Unchanged through all the ages. How long will
The mother grieve, and the hawk circle still?

1916

THE TWELVE

1.

Black night.
White snow.
    The wind, the wind!
It all but lays you low.
    The wind, the wind,
Across God's world it blows!

    The wind is weaving
    The white snow.
There is ice below.
    Stumbling and tumbling,
    Folk slip and fall.
God pity all!

    From house to house
    A rope is strung,
    A sagging placard on it hung:
"All power to the Constituent Assembly!"

A bent old woman, tearful, trembly,
Stares at the placard in despair.
    Her blear eyes see
    How many fine foot-clouts could be
Cut from the canvas wasted there,
    While the children's feet go bare. . . .

    Like a hen she picks her way
Across the snow-blocked thoroughfare.
    "Oh, Mother of God, look down and see—
    "Those Bolsheviks will be the death of me!"

    The wind lashes at the crossing
    And the frost stings to the bone.

With his nose stuck in his collar
A *bourzhooy* * stands all alone.

And who is this? He has long hair
And mutters with a wrathful air:
   "Renegades!
   Russia is dead!"
A writer chap, no doubt, who has
    A glib tongue in his head. . . .

And here, slinking through the snow
Comes a cassock, black and bulky. . . .
Comrade priest,
   Why so sulky?

You used to strut—
Do you recall?
Your belly with its pendent cross
Shining on one and all.

A lady wrapped in caracul
   Turns to confide
To a companion: "Oh, we cried and cried . . ."
   She slips—and smack!
She's flat upon her back!

   Oh, oh, oh!
Lift her up, so!

The restive wind flirts,
A gay, cruel clown,
Wringing the skirts,
Mowing men down.

* A form of "bourgeois"; this slang term is used contemptuously of a
member of the exploiting middle-class.

Fierce-fisted, it kneads
The big placard that reads:
"All power to the Constituent Assembly."
  A gust wafts the words:

. . . Sure, we had a meeting too . . .
. . . In that building just ahead . . .
  . . . We were divided,
  But we decided:
Ten for a spell, twenty-five for the night,
  A copeck less wouldn't be right . . .
    . . . Let's go to bed . . .

  It's getting late.
  An empty street.
  Only a poor dead beat
  Goes past with shuffling gait.
And the wind wails.

Come here,
  Poor dear,
Give us a kiss!

  Bread!
What's ahead?
  Get along!

Darkness, darkness overhead.

Hate, sorrowful hate
  Bursts the heart . . .
Black, holy hate . . .

  Hey, comrade,
  Look sharp!

2.

The wind is romping, the snowflakes dance,
In the night twelve men advance.

Black, narrow rifle straps,
Cigarettes, crumpled caps.

A convict's stripes would fit their backs,
Fires, fires mark their tracks. . . .

    Freedom, ho, freedom,
  Unhallowed, unblest!
    Rat-tat-tat!

It's freezing, comrades, freezing.

"Now Vanka's off with Katya, on a spree. . . ."
"The tart, her stocking's stuffed with *kerenki!*" *

"And Vanka's got into a game that pays."
"He's ditched us, he's in uniform these days."
"Well, Vanka, you bourzhooy bastard, you!"
"Just try and kiss my girl—you'll see who's who!"

    Freedom, ho, freedom,
  Unhallowed, unblessed!
  Vanka's with Katya . . .
    You know the rest.
    Rat-tat-tat!

Fires, fires mark their track,
Their rifle straps are gleaming black.

March to the revolution's pace!
We've a grim enemy to face!

* Bills issued in 1917 while Kerensky headed the Provisional government.

Comrades, show spunk, take aim, the lot!
At Holy Russia let's fire a shot,

> At hutted Russia,
> Fat-rumped and solid,

Russia the stolid!

Eh, eh, unhallowed, unblessed!

3.

Our boys they marched away
To serve in the Red Army,
To serve in the Red Army—
It's do or die today!

Eh, what bitter sorrow!
  A sweet life we've won!
A ragged overcoat,
An Austrian gun!

It's all up with exploiters now.
We'll set the world on fire, we vow,
Flaming, flaming amidst blood—
  Bless us, Lord God!

4.

Whirling snow. "Halloo, my bloods!"
Vanka with his Katya scuds,
Two electric lanterns winking
  On the wagon shafts . . .
  Clear the way!

Uniformed, the dandy dashes,
Silly fool whom nothing fashes,
How he twirls his black moustaches,

Twirls, and teases,
    Sure he pleases . . .
Look at Vanka: he's got shoulders!
Listen: Vanka knows the game!
He is grabbing hold of Katya,
Trying to get round the dame.

Now she lifts her face, the girl's
Parted lips show teeth like pearls.
"Ho, Katya, my Katya,
Chubby mug!"

5.

"On your neck, my little Katya,
The knife scored a mark still fresh;
There are scratches on the flesh
Under your left breast, my Katya.

    Eh, eh, dance for me!
    You've a pair of legs, I see!

You used to go a pretty pace,
Wearing linen trimmed with lace;
You used to whore with the gold-braid crew—
Whore then, and get along with you!

    Eh, eh, whore all you wish—
    You make my heart leap like a fish!

Say, recall that officer,
Katya—how I knifed the cur?
Don't tell me your memory's vague,
Just refresh your wits, you plague.

    Eh, eh, refresh me, too,
    Come and let me sleep with you.

In gray gaiters you went 'round,
Gobbled chocolates by the pound,
Promenaded with cadets,
Now plain troopers are your pets.
    Eh, eh, little tart,
      Sin away and ease your heart.

6.

. . . The stallion gallops past again,
The driver, shouting, gives him rein.

"Andrukha, stop them, hold the horse!"
"Run back, Petrukha! Cut their course!"

Crrack-crack-crack! Crrack-crack-crack!
The snow leaps up and eddies back.

The sleigh and Vanka are out of sight.
"Now cock the gun again, wheel right!"

Crrack! "You'd better watch your game:

.   .   .   .

Stealing another fellow's dame!"

"The rat is gone. But I know who
Tomorrow will be quits with you."

And where is Katya? "Dead. She's dead!
The pretty slut shot through the head!

Happy, Katya? Don't you crow?
You carrion, lie there in the snow. . . ."

March to the revolution's pace.
We've a grim enemy to face.

7.

And again the twelve go marching,
Shoulders back and guns in place,
Only he, the poor assassin,
Marching, does not show his face.

Forward, forward, stepping faster,
Marching with a reckless tread,
Like a dog without a master,
Muffled up, he strides ahead.

"Comrade, what on earth has got you?
Why is it you act so dumb?"
"Spill it, Pyotr, is it Katya
Makes you look so God-dam' glum?"

"Well, comrades, you know the story.
Katya was my girl by rights.
Yes, I loved her. God, our roaring
Black and drunken summer nights!

Her bright eyes—they drove me to it—
How they dared you, black as coal!
And her shoulder, well I knew it
With its poppy-colored mole. . . .
I, mad fool, I had to do it,
Went and killed her . . . damn my soul. . . ."

"Listen to the bastard's patter!
Pyotr, are you a woman? Pooh!
Is your spirit soft as batter?
Got no guts, you donkey, you?
Come, friend, cut this silly chatter.
Take yourself in hand, man, do!"

"Comrade, we cannot be nursing
You or anyone just now.

Quit your glooming and your cursing.
Stiffer loads won't make us bow!"

Pyotr moves at a slower pace
And he shows a careless face,

Once again he lifts his head,
And his eyes grow bright.

Hi! Hi! What a din!
Sure, a bit of fun's no sin!

Lock your doors and windows tight!
There are looters out tonight!

Burst the cellars—wine is free!
Tonight the rabble's on the spree!

8.

Oh, the bitter sorrow!
Dullness, wearying,
Deadly!

My time
I will pass, I will pass.

My pate
I will scratch, I will scratch.

Sunflower seeds
I will crack.

With my knife
I will rip, I will rip.

Fly like a sparrow, bourzhooy.
I'll drink to my dead little dove,

To my black-browed love
In your blood. . . .
God rest the soul of thy servant, Katerina . . .

Ugh! I'm fed up!

9.

The city's roar has died away,
All's quiet on the Neva's brink.*
No more police! We can be gay,
Fellows, without a drop to drink.

A bourzhooy, standing at the crossing,
Nose in his collar, does not stir,
While, tail between his legs, beside him
Shivers a cringing, mangy cur.

The bourzhooy like a silent question
Stands there, starved: a dog that begs—
The old world like a kinless mongrel
Behind him, tail between its legs.

10.

How it's blowing! How it's snowing!
    The flakes blind you as they fly.
You can't see where you are going
    Through the blizzard whistling by.
Funnel-shaped, the snow swirls high,
Pillar-like against the sky.

"Saviour, here's a blizzard!" "What!
Pyotr, you're a dunderhead—
Did your Saviour and His kin
Save you from committing sin?
Pyotr, you are talking rot!

* This opening is a variant of lines from an old Russian song.

Whose fault is it Katya's dead?
You're a murderer—understand?
There is blood upon your hand!"
March to the revolution's pace:
We've a grim enemy to face!

On and on the steady beat
Of the workers' marching feet! *

11.

. . . And the twelve, unblessed, unhallowed,
Still go marching on,
Ready for what chance may offer,
Pitying none. . . .

On, with rifles lifted
At the unseen enemy.
Through dead alleys where the snow has sifted,
Where the blizzard tosses free.
Onward, where the snow has drifted
Clutching at the marcher's knee.

The red flag
Whips their faces.

Creaking snow,
Measured paces.

The grim foe
Marks their traces.

Day and night the blizzard flings
Snow that stings
In their faces.

* Variant of the refrain of a revolutionary song popular in the early
years of the century.

On, the steady beat
Of the workers' marching feet.

12.

. . . Onward as a haughty host they march.
"Hey! Who else is there? Come out!"
Only wind, wind bellying the flag,
Tossing the red flag about.

Up ahead a snowdrift towers sheer.
"Who is hiding in the drift? Come out!"
A starved mongrel shambles in the rear,
Limping off as though he feared a clout.

"Skip! D'you want your mangy fur
Tickled by this bayonet?
The old world is a mongrel cur. . . .
Beatings are the best you'll get."

. . . Teeth bared, gleaming in a wolfish grin,
Furtively it follows on behind,
A chilled mongrel, without friend or kin. . . .
"Hey! Who goes there? Answer quickly, mind!"

"Who's waving the red flag?" "Just try and see.
Lord, what darkness! and what blinding snow!"
"Who are those that run there stealthily,
Clinging to the houses as they go?"

"We will get you and your comrades too!
Best surrender while you're breathing still."
"Comrade . . . it will be the worse for you.
Come out! or we'll shoot to kill."

Crrack-crack-crack! A solitary
Echo answers, from the houses thrown,
While the blizzard, wild and merry,
Laughs among the snows alone.

Crrack-crack-crack!
Crrack-crack-crack!
. . . Forward as a haughty host they tread.
A starved mongrel shambles in the rear.
Bearing high the banner, bloody red,
    That He holds in hands no bullets sear—
    Hidden as the flying snow veils veer,
Lightly walking on the wind, as though
He Himself were diamonded snow,
    With mist-white roses garlanded:
    Jesus Christ is marching at their head.

1918

THE SCYTHIANS

Panmongolism—a slogan quite bizarre,
But none the less like music to my ear.
    —Vladimir Solovyov

You are the millions, we are multitude
And multitude and multitude.
Come, fight! Yea, we are Scythians,
Yea, Asians, a slant-eyed, greedy brood.

For you—the centuries, for us—one hour.
Like slaves, obeying and abhorred,
We were the shield between the breeds
Of Europe and the raging Mongol horde.

For centuries the hammers of your forge
Drowned out the avalanche's boom;
You heard like wild, fantastic tales
Of Lisbon's and Messina's sudden doom.

For centuries your eyes were toward the East.
Our pearls you hoarded in your chests
And mockingly you bode the day
When you could aim your cannon at our breasts.

The time has come. Disaster beats its wings.
Each day the insults grow apace.
The hour will strike, and it may chance
Your Paestums will go down and leave no trace.

Oh, pause, old world, while life still beats in you,
Oh, weary one, oh, worn, oh, wise!
Halt here, as once did Oedipus
Before the Sphinx's enigmatic eyes.

Yea, Russia is a Sphinx. Exulting, grieving,
And sweating blood, she cannot sate
Her eyes that gaze and gaze and gaze
At you with stone-lipped love for you, and hate.

Yea, you have long since ceased to love
As our hot blood can love; the taste
You have forgotten of a love
That burns like fire and like fire lays waste.

All things we love: pure numbers' burning chill,
The visions that divinely bloom;
All things we know: the Gallic light
And the parturient Germanic gloom.

And we remember all: Parisian hells,
The cool of Venice's lagoons,
Far fragrance of green lemon groves,
And Cologne's masses that the smoke festoons.

And flesh we love, its color and its taste,
Its deathy odor, heavy, raw.
And is it our guilt if your bones
May crack beneath our powerful supple paw?

It is our wont to seize wild colts at play:
They rear and impotently shake
Wild manes—we crush their mighty croups.
And shrewish women slaves we tame—or break.

Come unto us from the black ways of war,
Come to our peaceful arms and rest.
Comrades, before it is too late,
Sheathe the old sword; may brotherhood be blest.

If not, we have not anything to lose.
We too can practice perfidies.
By sick descendants you will be
Accursed for centuries and centuries.

To welcome pretty Europe, we shall spread
And scatter in the tangled space
Of our wide thickets. We shall turn
To you our alien Asiatic face.

Go, all of you, to Ural fastnesses;
We clear the ground for the appalling scenes
Of war between the savage Mongol hordes
And pitiless science with its massed machines.

Know that we will no longer be your shield
But, careless of the battle cries,
We'll watch the deadly duel seethe,
Aloof, with indurate and narrow eyes.

We will not move when the ferocious Hun
Despoils the corpse and leaves it bare,
Burns towns, herds cattle in the church,
And smell of white flesh roasting fills the air.

For the last time, old world, we bid you rouse,
For the last time the barbarous lyre sounds
That calls you to our bright fraternal feast
Where labor beckons and where peace abounds.

[*1918*]

Maximilian Voloshin

CIMMERIAN TWILIGHT

I.

The evening light has soaked with ancient gold
And gall the hills. Like strips of tawny fur,
The tufts of shaggy grass glow ruddier;
Past fiery bushes metal waves unfold;
Piled boulders, naked cliffs the sea has holed
Show enigmatic fronts that lour and blur.
In the winged twilight figures seem to stir:
A huge paw looms, a jowl grins stark and bold,
Like swelling ribs the dubious hillocks show;
On what bent back, like wool, does savory grow?
What brute, what titan, to this region cleaves?
The dark is strange . . . and yonder, space is clean.
And there the weary ocean, panting, heaves,
And rotting grasses breathe of iodine.

II.

Here stood a sacred forest. Here moved the divine
Wing-footed messenger, whose passing brushed the glades.
Cities stood here: their ruin's mere remembrance fades,
Where now only the sheep graze on the burnt incline.
Sharp-etched the peaks! Their toothed crowns catch the shine
As the green dusk, eerily sad, invades.
Whose timeless anguish stings my soul as with edged blades?
Who knows the road of gods? The start and the decline?
The churning rubble grinds and groans as long before;
Against the sandbanks of the wide and echoing shore,
Lifting its heavy crests, the troubled ocean fumes;
And starry nights drop their slow tears into the sea . . .
While outcast gods, whose faces light no more illumes,
Gaze and demand and summon inescapably.

170

III.

Above the rocking waters' ripples fiercely stand
Deep-rooted crests: a desert ridge of craggy stubble;
Black precipices frown on torrents of red rubble—
The grievous reaches of an inscrutable land.
In the sad, solemn dreams that haunt me I have found
A lost land's echoing bays where, as late dusk is falling,
More sorrowfully and more musically calling,
Forsaken waves in waste hexameters resound.
And gliding on that pathlessness as on a river
Of darkness, a sail floats with the mysterious quiver
Of anguished winds and of the deep that heaves and fails.
Thrust by the seas' blind push, my fated skiff is going
Forth where the road of daring and of penance hails,
While lamplike in the sky the Seven Stars are glowing.

LUNARIA

XV.°

Pure pearl of silence brooding on the sky,
Presider o'er conception, lamp of dreams,
Love's crystal, altar where night's mystery gleams,
Queen of the waters where thou lov'st to lie,
From the damp depths, with what a plaintive sigh,
Through my dark crucifixions toward thy beams,
O Dian, O fierce Hecate, there streams
Vision on vision, unlived, snakelike, shy.

How sweet yet weirdly joyless are the folds
And caves thy diamond delirium holds.
The flashing mica of thy empty seas

° *This concludes a cycle of fifteen sonnets, so written that the last line of each forms the first line of the next, the final sonnet being composed of the first lines of the preceding fourteen.*

In listless ether shows like horror's face,
Thou frozen cry that nothing can appease,
Thou dead world's avid corpse, cast out on space.

1913

TERROR

They worked at night, they went through
Reports, dockets, depositions.
They signed sentences hurriedly.
They yawned. And drank.
In the morning they served out vodka to the soldiers.
In the evening, by candlelight,
Those listed, men and women, were summoned,
And driven into a dark courtyard.
Their clothing, shoes, linen, were removed
And tied into bundles
That were loaded onto trucks and carted off.
The rings and watches they shared among themselves.
At night they drove the barefoot and the hungry
Over icy ground,
With a northeaster blowing,
To the vacant outskirts of the city.
With rifle butts they pushed them to the gully's edge,
Snapping on their flashlights.
The machine guns worked half a minute.
Those not mown down they did for with bayonets.
Some were thrown into the pit alive.
Earth was flung in hastily.
Then, marching to a spacious Russian song,
They returned to town.
At dawn wives, mothers, dogs
Made their way to the gully.
They dug up the earth, they quarreled over bones,
They kissed the beloved flesh.

1920

UNDER SAIL

Five days we have been cruising, nor once have furled
The bellying sails.
Nights have been spent in bays,
In coves and estuaries,
Where a full moon blossomed above the dunes.
By day the wind drives us along the shallow
And lonely sandbanks,
Seething with white foam.
Stayed by the carven rudder,
I watch
From the high prow
The dance of the deck;
The massed seas shimmer, and beyond,
The interlacing rigging frames
The untenanted ocean.
A balked wave's splash,
A taut mast's creak,
A gurgling underneath the prow—
And one still sail . . .
Behind—the city,
All a red ecstasy
Of spilling flags,
Inflamed with fear and anger,
Chill with rumors,
Quivering with hope,
Tortured by hunger,
Plagues and blood—
City where tardy Spring glides stealthily,
In a lace veil of flowers and acacias.
But here—only the windless, soundless, unplumbed deep.
The sky, the water, are two valves
Of a vast pearl shell.
The sun is caught in cobweb rays.
The ship in cloudy spaces hangs,

In blunt and smoky splendor.
Yonder is seen the shore of your bare land
Of wormwood, drought, and stone—
Your land fatigued
With being the thoroughfare of tribes and peoples.
I shall set you as a witness to their madness,
And I shall lead you by a bladelike path,
That you may bear within you the immense
Silence of the twilit, shimmering sea.

1923

Vladislav Khodasevich

THE MONKEY

The day was hot. The forests were on fire.
Time dragged. Behind the country house next door
A cock was crowing. The gate swung behind me.
There on a bench, leaning against the fence,
A wandering Serb, lean, swarthy, had dozed off.
A heavy cross, fashioned of silver, hung
On his half-naked breast, down which great drops
Of sweat were rolling. On the fence, close by,
A small red-skirted monkey crouched, and chewed
The dusty leaves of lilac overhead.
A leather collar on a heavy chain
That pulled her back pressed hard against her throat.
The Serb, roused by my step, awoke and wiped
His sweat, and begged some water for the creature.
He tasted it, to test how cold it was,
Then placed the saucer on the bench. At once
The monkey, wetting eager fingers, seized
The saucer in both hands. She leaned her elbows
Upon the bench, and crouching thus, she drank.
Her chin was almost resting on the boards,
And her back arched above her half-bald pate.
Even so Darius, centuries ago,
Fleeing the phalanxes of Alexander,
Must have leaned to a puddle in the road.
When she had drunk her water, casually
The monkey brushed the saucer off the bench,
And standing up, with an immortal gesture
She offered me her small black horny hand
The moisture had left cool. . . .
Though I have pressed the hands of lovely women,
Of poets, and of men who led a nation,

Yet there was not one hand among them all
Had such a noble shape. Not any hand
Ever touched mine in such full comradeship!
I swear by God that no one ever looked
Into my eyes so wisely and so deeply;
Her soft gaze pierced me. That indigent creature
Revived for me the sweetest lore bequeathed
By far antiquity to human hearts.
And in that moment life appeared so full,
It seemed to me the sun and moon, the waves
Of all the seas, the winds, the heavenly spheres,
Were choiring together, organ music
That rang as wonderfully in my ears
As in the days beyond man's memory.
And then the Serb, knuckling his tambourine,
Went off, the monkey perched on his left shoulder:
A maharajah on an elephant.
And in the heavens, wreathed in opal smoke,
A swollen, raspberry-colored sun was hanging.
Heat, with no hope of thunder, lay upon
The wheat fields that were wilting in the blaze.
That was the very day war was declared.

1919

THE CORK

O cork that stoppered the strong iodine,
How rapidly you rotted quite away!
Thus is the body quietly consumed,
Burnt by the soul, unseen, day after day.

1921

"IT SCARCELY SEEMS WORTH WHILE"

It scarcely seems worth while to sing, to live:
Uncouth, unsafe, the days through which we crawl.
The tailor sews, the builder rears his beams;
The seams will come apart, the house will fall.

But then through this corruption suddenly
I hear sometimes, how moved to feel it true,
Astir and throbbing in that rotten frame,
A different life, one altogether new.

Just so, enduring her routine dull days,
A woman restlessly will lift and press
Her hand against her belly's swelling weight
With what a swift astonished tenderness.

1922

Lubov Stolitza

LENT

In thaws like cloth-of-gold blithe noonday goes,
While midnight wraps herself in silver snows.
The aspen buds show rosy as a shell
On boughs where diamond hoarfrost glints as well.
My gentle puss furtively slipped away,
But on my sill a swallow perched today.
The woes of winter dwindle and depart,
But now spring griefs are knocking at the heart.
At noon, in church, sister and I must weep,
At midnight, flushed with heat, we lie asleep,
Knees pressed together, brows serenely wise,
But oh, the shadows, blue under our eyes!

Zinaida Shishova

"AN UNFAMILIAR AIR"

An unfamiliar air, O God, possesses
Your earth today.
Beyond the window, strangely like acacias,
The poplars sway.

I draw my hand from out my muff and find it
Grown hot and dry.
And from my furs, as though May touched them lightly,
Faint perfumes fly.

And all night long dark dreams rise up to haunt me,
They choke and cling.
How then shall I forbear at last from fearing,
O God, your spring?

Ivan Bunin

"THE HOPS"

The hops already have sere leaves to show
Along the fences, and beyond the farms
In gardens where the light, its heat now spent,
Lies mellow-bright, the great bronze melons glow.

The grain has all been hauled away. You catch
A glimpse, above a hut out on the steppe,
Of a gray windmill with a lifted wing
That shines against the sky, a golden patch.

[1903]

RUSSIAN SPRING

In the valley the birches are bored.
On the meadows, a dingy fog.
Sodden, with horse dung floored,
The highroad is bleak as a bog.

From the village asleep on the plains
Comes the odor of fresh-baked bread.
Two tramps with their packs are at pains
To limp on till they come to a bed.

Spring mud is thick on the streets
Where puddles gleam in the sun.
Steam drifts from damp earthen seats;
The fumes from the oven stun.

The sheep dog, dragging his chain,
Yawns on the barn-door sill.

Indoors there is reek and stain.
The haze-wrapped steppe is still.

The carefree cocks perform
For spring, till the day is spent.
The meadow is drowsy and warm,
The glad heart indolent.

[1905]

FLAX

She sits upon the tumulus and stares,
Old woman Death, down at the crowded road.
Like a blue flame the small flax-flower flares,
Thick through the meadows sowed.

And says old woman Death: "Hey, traveler!
Does anyone want linen, linen fit
For funeral wear? A shroud, madam or sir,
I'll take cheap coin for it."

The mound remains serene: "Don't crow so loud!"
It says, "The winding sheet is dust and cracks
And crumbles into earth, that from the shroud
May spring the sky-blue flax."

[1907]

THE NEW CHURCH

A fresh spring gust blew down upon us
Across the altars, new and clean,
And someone overhead dripped whitewash
Upon the golden icon screen.

Sonorous noise roamed round the columns.
In smocks, our brushes lifted high,
We climbed the scaffolding, and upward
Into the cupola—the sky.

The plasterers would sing together
With us. Not in the common way
We painted Christ, Who listened to us
In the new church, so bright and gay.

Our simple songs, we thought, would take Him
Back to the sunlight on the floor
At Nazareth, back to the workbench,
And the blue tunic that He wore.

[1907]

A SONG

I'm a plain girl whose hands are stained with earth,
He is a fisherman—he's gay and keen.
His far white sail is sinking in the firth.
Many the seas and rivers he has seen.

The women of the Bosphorus, they say,
Are good-looking . . . and I—I'm lean and black.
The white sail sinks far out beyond the bay.
It may be that he never will come back.

I will wait on in good and evil weather.
If vainly, take my wage, go to the sea
And cast the ring and hope away together.
And my black braid will serve to strangle me.

IN AN EMPTY HOUSE

The blue wallpaper has lost its hue,
Gone daguerreotypes and icons, too—
Only where they hung for many years
The old blue in patches now appears.

Now forgotten, now forgotten quite
Much that once was all the heart's delight.
Those alone who will not come again,
Those have left a trace that will remain.

[*1916*]

Nikolay Gumilyov

EVENING

With heaviness this wingless wind is cursed,
The sunset is a melon that has burst.

You ache to give the clouds a gentle shove,
They float so indolently up above.

Upon such languid evenings you will see
Coachmen whip up their horses savagely,

And fishers tear the waters with the oar,
And woodsmen batter at the oaks they floor. . . .

While those who in their being must rehearse
The movement of the throbbing universe,

Who house within them, slumbering or astir,
Rhythms to come and all that ever were,

Write winged verses whose resistless sweep
Rouses the sluggard elements from sleep.

1916

BLACK DIAMOND

Black velvet where a shining diamond
Forgotten lies,
To that I can compare the look that nigh
Sings in her eyes.

Her porcelain body's whiteness is too vague,
Too sweet a boon,
Like a white lilac blossom dim beneath
A dying moon.

Within her soft and waxen hands the blood
Burns hot and bright
As an eternal candle set within
The Virgin's sight.

And all of her is airy as a bird
That would fly forth
On a clear day in autumn, taking leave
Of the sad North.

1918

SECOND CANZONE

We are not in the world at all, but somewhere
Out in the world's backyard, amid a maze
Of shadowy nothings. Drowsily the summer
Leafs through the broad blue pages of clear days.

The pendulum, callous and conscientious,
Time's fiancé, still undiscomfited
Though unacknowledged, takes the scheming seconds
And deftly slices off each pretty head.

So parched lies every road here and so dusty,
And so does every shrub for dryness strain,
That a white seraph will not meet us, leading
A unicorn sedately by the rein.

And only in your secret sorrow, darling,
Is there a fiery opiate to stay
The curse of this sad place of desolation,
Like a fair wind from countries far away.

Where all is brilliance, all is movement, singing,
And soft enchantment to the eye and ear—
There is it that we live! A stagnant cistern
Has prisoned only our reflection here.

1921

Mikhail Zenkevich

"BELATED SUNFLOWERS"

Belated sunflowers smoldered in the meadow,
And, in the sapphire of the sky inlaid,
The curve of a hawk's wing luxuriated
In the mild heat and glittered like a blade.

And setting bounds to mortal man's desiring,
Above the stubble of the fields Fate sped
Behind us like a disembodied shadow
Of the sharp wing that glided overhead.

Magnificent and languid as this noonday,
Taming the rising heat, you strode with ease.
Alone your skirts frothed in a foam of laces,
Beating against your proud and stately knees.

And in your wide eyes that were faintly misted,
Ready to swoop upon the doomed, a mite
Of sultriness immobile on the azure,
Passion showed hawklike, gleaming dark and bright.

1916

Osip Mandelstamm

"THE AIR STRIKES CHILL"

The air strikes chill. Although transparent spring
Has clothed Petropolis in pale green down,
The Neva's waves are faintly sickening
As if they were Medusa's coiling crown.
On the embankment of our northern stream
The fireflies of hurrying motors gleam.
Steel dragonflies and beetles flit and whirr,
And stars are pins of gold whose glitter pricks,
But stars can never mortally transfix
The heavy emerald of the sea water.

1916

"ON EVERY STILL SUBURBAN STREET"

On every still suburban street
The gatekeepers are shoveling snow;
A passer-by, I do not know
The bearded peasants whom I meet.

The kerchiefed women come and go,
There's yelping from some crazy tike,
In tea house and in home alike
The samovars' red roses glow.

THE TWILIGHT OF LIBERTY

Come, brothers, hail this great and twilight year,
Come, celebrate the dusk of liberty.
The nets, a jungle of them, are let down

Into a savage, dark, nocturnal sea.
Bleak is the season in which you arise,
O sun, O people in your sovereignty.

Come, celebrate the fateful burden, see
What our grave leader now assumes with tears:
Exalt and hail the dark burden of power,
Weighted with black oppression through the years
O time, your ship is splitting and it sinks:
There is no one who has a heart but hears.

We have pressed swallows into service, birds
Battle for us in winged legions—lo!
The sun cannot be seen, the whole air heaves,
It twitters, trembles, lives, moves on, although
The nets are strong, the dusk is thick, the sun
Cannot be seen, earth swims upon the flow.

Well, then let's try it, give the rudder one
Huge, clumsy, creaking turn. For all you're worth,
Pull! Earth swims forward. Courage, men! Lift up
The load of grief, for this road knows no mirth;
We'll yet recall when Lethe chills our bones
The price we paid: ten heavens for this earth.

1918

Anna Akhmatova

CONFESSION

Silence: now he has shriven me.
In lilac dusk the taper smolders;
The dark stole's rigid drapery
Conceals a massive head and shoulders.

"Talitha kumi": is it He
Once more? How fast the heart is beating. . . .
A touch: a hand moves absently
The customary cross repeating.

[*1911*]

"BROAD GOLD"

Broad gold, the evening heavens glow,
The April air is cool and tender.
You should have come ten years ago,
And yet in welcome I surrender.

Come here, sit closer to me, look
With eyes that twinkle, mouth that purses
Into the little blue-bound book
That hold my awkward childish verses.

Forgive me that I long forsook
Joy's sunny paths, nor glanced toward any;
Forgive me those whom I mistook
For you—alas, they were too many.

[*1915*]

189

PRAYER

Make me feverish, sleepless, and breathless,
Let the years of prostration be long,
O Lord, take my child and companion,
And destroy the sweet power of song.

Thus I pray at each matins, each vespers,
After these many wearying days,
That the storm cloud which lowers over Russia
May be changed to a nimbus ablaze.

[1915]

"LIKE A WHITE STONE"

Like a white stone deep in a draw-well lying,
As hard and clear, a memory lies in me.
I cannot strive nor have I heart for striving:
It is such pain and yet such ecstasy.

It seems to me that some one looking closely
Into my eyes would see it, patent, pale;
And seeing, would grow sadder and more thoughtful
Than one who listens to a bitter tale.

The ancient gods changed men to things, but left them
A consciousness that smoldered endlessly.
That marvelous sorrows might endure forever,
You have been changed into a memory.

[1916]

"UPON THE HARD CREST"

Upon the hard crest of a snowdrift
We tread, and grown quiet, we walk

On towards my house, white, enchanted;
Our mood is too tender for talk.

And sweeter than song is this dream now
Come true, the low boughs of the firs
That sway as we brush them in passing,
The slight silver clink of your spurs.

                                [1917]

"ALL IS SOLD"

All is sold, all is lost, all is plundered,
Death's wing has flashed black on our sight,
All's gnawed bare with sore want and sick longing—
Then how are we graced with this light?

By day there's a breath of wild cherry
In the city, from woods none espies;
At night new and strange constellations
Shine forth in the pale summer skies.

And these houses, this dirt, these mean ruins,
Are touched by the miracle, too;
It is close, the desired, despaired of,
That all longed for, but none ever knew.

                                [1921]

"AN UNPARALLELED AUTUMN"

An unparalleled autumn erected a glorious dome;
All the clouds were commanded to leave it undarkened and pure.
And men marveled: September is gone, and yet where are the days
Shot with dampness and chill? How long can this wonder endure?

                                                    191

In the turbid canals the mild waters shone emerald-clear,
And the nettles had fragrance more rich than the roses to give;
And the sunsets that laid on the air their unbearable weight
Of demoniac crimson, we shall not forget while we live.
Like a rebel who enters the capital: thus the proud sun,
Which this autumn like spring was so hungry to smile at and woo
That it seemed any moment a snowdrop, transparent, would gleam—
Then I saw, on the path to my door, stepping quietly, you.

[*1922*]

"REJECT THE BURDEN"

Reject the burden of all earthly solace,
Put from your heart the claims of home and wife;
Does your child hunger? Give unto a stranger
The bread that else would feed that little life.
Humble yourself to be the meanest servant
Of your worst enemy, and learn to call
The brute beast of the forest ways your brother,
And ask of God nothing, nothing at all.

1923

"NOT WITH DESERTERS"

Not with deserters from the battle
That tears my land do I belong.
To their coarse praise I do not listen.
They shall not have from me one song.

Poor exile, you are like a prisoner
To me, or one upon the bed
Of sickness. Dark your road, O wanderer,
Of wormwood smacks your alien bread.

192

Here, into smoking fires that blacken
Our lives, the last of youth we throw,
Who in the years behind us never
Sought to evade a single blow.

We know that in the final reckoning
No hour will need apology;
No people in the world are prouder,
More tearless, simpler, than are we.

1923

LOT'S WIFE

And he who was righteous loomed radiant, striding
Behind the Lord's messenger up the black hill.
But she walked reluctant—alarm spoke within her:
"It is not too late, you may look on it still,

Upon the vermilion-stained towers of Sodom;
You spun in that court, and you sang on that square;
That house whose tall windows confront you with blankness
Once knew you, a bride; you bore your sons there."

She turned to behold it, and pain was her master;
Her eyes yearning toward it could no longer see;
Salt-white grew her body, the blood in it withered;
Firm earth held her feet that would never go free.

And is there not one who would weep for this woman,
Or one who would find her loss bitter to brook?
Alone in my heart, uneclipsed, unforgotten,
Is she who gave over her life for one look.

1924

"OH, HOW GOOD"

Oh, how good the snapping and the crackle
Of the frost that daily grows more keen!
Laden with its dazzling icy roses,
The white-flaming bush is forced to lean.

On the snows in all their pomp and splendor
There are ski tracks, and it seems that they
Are a token of those distant ages
When we two together passed this way.

1940

COURAGE

What hangs in the balance is nowise in doubt;
We know the event and we brave what we know;
Our clocks are all striking the hour of courage—
That sound travels with us wherever we go.
To die of a bullet is nothing to dread,
To find you are roofless is easy to bear;
And all is endured, O great language we love:
It is you, Russian tongue, we must save, and we swear
We will give you unstained to the sons of our sons;
You shall live on our lips, and we promise you—never
A prison shall know you, but you shall be free
Forever.

1942

THE MISTRESS OF THE HOUSE

Once, before I came, a witch
Lived alone here in this room.
On the eve of the new moon
You may see her shadow loom.

Still her shadow falls across
The high threshold crookedly,
And, evasive but intent,
She looks sternly in at me.

I myself am not of those
By another's witchcraft caught.
I myself . . . but I do not
Give my secrets up for naught.

1946

Igor Severyanin

A RUSSIAN SONG

On the forest laces morning's pink is shed,
Shrewdly the small spider climbs his filmy thread.

Dews are diamonding and blooming faery-bright.
Oh, what golden air! What beauty! Oh, what light!

It is good to wander through the dawn-shot rye,
Good to see a bird, a toad, a dragonfly;

Good to catch the crowing of the sleepy cock,
And to laugh at echo, and to hear her mock.

Ah, I love to shout idly as I pass,
And among the shining birches glimpse a lass,

Glimpse, and leaning on the tangled fence, to chase
Dawn's unwilling shadows from her morning face.

Ah, to wake her from her half-surrendered sleep,
Tell her of my new-sprung dreams that soar and leap,

Hug her trembling breasts that press against my heart,
Stir the morning in her, hear its pulses start.

1910

SPRING APPLE TREE

(An Aquarelle)

An apple tree can grieve my spirit so,
Its branches whitely weighted with unmelting snow:
Thus might a hunchbacked girl stand, delicate and dumb,

196

As trembling the tree stands and strikes my genius numb. . . .
It looks into the wide, pale shallows, mirror-clear,
Seeking to shed the dews that stain it like a tear;
And stilled with horror, groans like a decrepit cart,
Seeing the dismal hunch mocked by the pool's bright art.
When steely sleep alights upon the silent lake,
To the bent apple tree, as for a sick girl's sake,
I come to offer tenderness the boughs would miss,
I press upon the petal-perfumed tree a kiss.
Then trustingly, with tears, the tree confides her care
To me, and with a gentle touch brushes my hair.
Her boughs encircle me, her little twigs enlace,
And I lift up my lips to kiss her flowering face.

1910

Velemir Khlebnikov

"ELEPHANTS FOUGHT"

Elephants fought with flashing tusks
So that they looked like white stone
Under a sculptor's hand.
Reindeer twined their antlers
So that they seemed linked by a marriage of long standing,
With respective infatuations and infidelities.
Rivers flowed into the sea
So that the hand of one seemed to clutch the throat of the other.

[*1910–11*]

Vladimir Mayakovsky

MOONLIT NIGHT

(A Landscape)

There will be a moon.
Already a bit of it
shows.
And now a full moon is hanging in the air.
It must be that God is fishing about
with a marvelous
silver spoon
in the star chowder.

1916

OUR MARCH

Slog the squares with rebel tramping!
Higher, crags of haughty heads!
We will wash the worlds' cities
With the surge of a second flood.

Brindled, the ox of days.
Slow, the dray of years.
Our god's Speed.
Our hearts—drums.

What heavenlier than our golds?
What bullet wasp can sting us?
Our weapons are our song.
Our gold—our roaring voices.

Meadow, gather your greens,
Line the lair of days.
Rainbow, furnish yokes
For the swift steeds of the years.

The starry sky is bored:
We have shut it out from our songs.
Hey, Great Dipper, demand
That they hoist us to heaven alive.

Drink to joy! Sing!
Spring has flooded our blood.
Heart, beat, leap!
Our breasts are crashing brass.

1918

THE WORKER POET

They yell at the poet:
"Well—let's see you at a lathe.
What's verse?
It's not worth a curse and you know it.
You haven't the guts for real work."
Maybe that we don't show it,
But maybe we
Love handwork above all else.
I'm a factory—see?
And if you chaps declare
That I have no smokestack, perhaps
I find it harder to be
Without smokestacks—get that?
I know
You don't like empty talk. You work
With hard stubborn wood.
And we—
Aren't we woodworkers too?
We hew
The wood of men's heads.
You bet

It's a good thing to fish,
It's fine to haul in a net
Bouncing with sturgeon! But
The poet's work
I tell you is worthier yet.
His catch isn't fish, he hauls in
Human beings, friend.
It's great, I'll grant you, to tend
A furnace,
Fine to temper
The hissing iron bars.
But who is it disdains
Us, calls us loafers?
We with the rasp of the tongue
File not iron bars but brains.
Who stands higher then—
Poets or engineers?
Who gives men solid values?
Both.
Hearts are motors too.
The soul is a fine machine.
We two are peers,
Comrades of the working masses,
Proletarians of body and spirit,
Only together
Enriching the universe,
Making it march to music.
Come, let's build a breakwater
To save us from verbal storms.
Get on with the job, it's enormous—
Something alive and new!
As for the orators who haven't a thing to do,
There's no place for them on our beaches.
Off with them to the mills!
Let them turn millstones with the water of their speeches.

1918

A MOST EXTRAORDINARY ADVENTURE

That Befell Vladimir Mayakovsky in the Summer, at the Rumyantzov
Cottage, Mount Akula, Pushkino, on the Yaroslavl Railway

The sunset flamed: a hundred suns,
summer had wheeled into July,
the heavens stirred and blurred
with heat,
and it was in the country this occurred.
Pushkino sat
on Mount Akula's hump,
and at its foot
a village writhed, its clump
of roofs as warped as bark.
Now off beyond the village was
a hole,
and every day
the sun dropped down into that hole,
as slow as sure.
And every morrow,
the sun, as red
as ever, raised his head
to flood the world.
Dawn after dawn
it was the same,
till it began to pall upon
me, till
I just got sore.
One day, in such a rage
that everything grew pale and shook with fear,
I shouted right in the sun's face:
"Climb down! D'you hear?
Stop it—haunting that lousy pit!"
I yelled, right at the sun:
"You loafer!
You've a soft berth in the clouds,

while I must sit,
not knowing if it's winter, if it's summer,
just drawing posters!"
I yelled to the sun:
"You wait!
Listen to me, you golden-browed,
instead of setting as you always do,
why don't you come around," I cried out loud,
"and have a glass of tea
with me?"
What have I done!
Now I'm a goner!
Here's the sun
coming to call on me
himself,
and of his own free will!
His beamy legs flung wide,
the sun strides right across the hill.
Pretending I'm not scared,
I beat retreat.
His eyes are in the garden now,
he's tramping through the garden now.
Filling
the windows,
filling
doors and cracks,
the burly sun walked in,
just so—dropped in,
and having got his breath,
spoke in a great bass voice:
"I have to hold my fires in check
the first time since creation.
You've invited me?
Then, poet, get the tea!
And don't forget the jam."
And though I wept with heat

and dripped a flood of sweat,
I got the samovar.
"Well, have a seat,
friend luminary."
The devil must have made me shout
my impudences at the sun.
Abashed,
I sat on the chair's edge,
afraid of what was going to happen next!
But from the sun
a strange light flowed—
he didn't seem too vexed—
and I, forgetting my embarrassment,
no longer scary,
sat—
talking to the luminary!
I chat
of this and that,
saying Rosta * has got me down,
and the sun says:
"Oh, well,
don't fret,
just take it in your stride.
Do you believe
that it's a cinch for me
to shine?
You go and try!
But I—
I undertook the job
to light the earth:
well then, I shine for all I'm worth."
And so we chat until it's dark—
that is, till when night used to come.
What kind of darkness can there be,
when the sun's there?

* *Russian Telegraph Agency.*

Now, having become chummy, we
address each other quite familiarly.
And soon,
in open friendship, just like that,
I pat him on the back.
And then the sun says—not to be outdone:
"Well, comrade, I declare,
we are a pair!
Let's go, poet,
let's soar,
and sing to scare
the drabness of the world.
I'll pour out light,
you'll do no worse
in pouring forth your verse."
At that the sun lets fly a cannon ball:
the prison wall
of nights falls flat.
Rays and words,
shine for all you're worth!
And when the sun gets tired,
and night, the stupid sleepyhead,
wants to drop off,
suddenly I am fired
with zeal, and shine for all I'm worth,
and day rings forth again.
Always to shine,
and to the very last
to shine,
and let the rest go hang;
thus runs
my motto and the sun's!

1920

From THE TALE OF HOW FADEY LEARNED
OF THE LAW PROTECTING WORKINGMEN °

Fadey had fought on every front
And helped the Commune as a soldier can.
He'd shed
              whole bucketfuls
                                of blood.
And now
          he's home again,
                            a workingman.
He looked at Moscow,
                      and at all the folk.
And then he scratched his pate and spoke:
"I've got to earn my bread," says he,
"But here is Nep—†
                    what will become of me?
Once more I'll have to stand,
                              waiting, hat in hand.
And then the boss
                  will hire another, to my loss.
Oh, damn it all to hell!
The goose hangs high—
                      and all I get's the smell!"
Prov cut him short:
                    "Come, that's enough.
Why are you handing out such stuff?
Today
      we manage things another way;

° *This piece was written to order for the Moscow local of the Printers'*
Union. The contract called for the composition of "a poem in verse pop-
ularizing the Code of Labor Laws," and it was stipulated that Comrade
Mayakovsky "convey in a poetic and artistic form the exact meaning
of the articles of the Code indicated by the Union." The end product
was the result of collective effort, Mayakovsky collaborating with several
fellow poets.
† *New Economic Policy which partially reinstated private enterprise.*

You can't just hire
                   whom you like—then fire.
You cannot pick
                   workmen out of the air.
Go to the Labor Exchange, get them there."
"Good heavens!"
                   growls Fadey.
And Prov says: "Scratch your pate!" and grins:
"Today it is the workingman who wins.
It's not the boss who hires and fires—
                                            times change:
The cur has got to bow
                   to the Exchange!"

                                            1924

From HOME!*

I don't want
                   to be plucked like a flower
in a meadow
                   after working hours.
I want
          the Gosplan †
                   to sweat, debating
my production quota
                   for the year.
I want
          the commissar of the times
                                    to lean
over my thought with an order.

* *The poem was written just after Mayakovsky's return from the United States, at the end of 1925. The 14th Congress of the Communist Party was then in session. The political report of the Central Committee was presented by Stalin.*
† *State Planning Commission.*

I want
        my heart's ration of love
to be the extra one
                allotted to specialists.
I want
        the shop committee
                        when my work is done
to secure my lips
                with a padlock.
I want
        the pen to be equal
                        to the bayonet.
I want
        Stalin
                representing the Politbureau
to report
        on the output of verse
as he does
        on the output
                        of pig iron and steel:
"Out of workingmen's
                hovels
we've climbed
                to the top;
in the Union
        of Republics
                        the appreciation of poetry
has surpassed
        the prewar level. . . ."

1925

SO WHAT?

I made the newssheets rustle, opening
Their eyes that blinked.

And suddenly
From every frontier
                    the gunpowder smell
Came stinging home to me.
For those past twenty
                    it is nothing new
To grow where tempests rage.
                              We are not glad,
Of course, but then what cause
Have we got to be sad?
The seas of history
                    are rough.
These threats,
            these wars, we'll brave,
And break into the open,
                        cutting them
As a keel cleaves
                the wave.

1927

HEINESQUE

Her eyes flashed lightning:
"I saw you
with another woman.
You are the lowest,
the vilest creature . . ."
And she went on
and on
and on, scolding. . . .
I'm a learned chap, darling,
quit thundering.
If your lightning did not strike me dead,
then, by God, your thunder
won't scare me.

From AT THE TOP OF MY VOICE

1.

My verse will reach you

                across the range of ages

and over the heads

                of poets and premiers.

My verse will reach you,

                but not in this wise:

not like an arrow

                in venery,

not the way a worn coin

                reaches a numismatist,

not like the light from a dead star.

My verse

        by its labor

                will pierce the mountain of years,

and appear

        visible,

           tangible,

                massive,

as an aqueduct

        built by Roman slaves

enters

    our days.

Finding by chance,

                in barrows of books

where verse lies buried,

the iron lines,

touch them

        with respect

like old,

        but terrible weapons.

2.

Let fame,

        like a comfortless

widow,

Walk behind genius
                    in funeral processions;
You, my verse,
                die like a common soldier,
As in an attack our men
                        died their anonymous deaths.

I spit
        on tons of bronze,
I spit
        on marble offal.
As for fame,
                we'll square accounts amicably—
Sharing one monument:
Socialism
            built
                in battle.

1930

"IT'S TWO O'CLOCK" *

It's two o'clock. You are in bed already.
A silvery Oka: the Milky Way.
I'm in no hurry; why wake and disturb you
With telegrams' electrical display?
The game's played out now, as they say, the vessel
Of love smashed on existence, if you please.
We've settled our accounts. And there's no reason
In listing mutual pains, griefs, injuries.
Just see how still it is. Night lays a starry
Tax on the sky. You get up and converse,
At such an hour as this, with all the ages,
With history, and with the universe.

1930

* *Mayakovsky's last poem. Lines 5–8 were inserted in the letter that the poet wrote just before committing suicide, except that "We've settled our accounts" was changed to "I have settled accounts with life."*

211

Boris Pasternak

"THE DROWSY GARDEN"

The drowsy garden scatters insects
Bronze as the ash from braziers blown.
Level with me and with my candle,
Hang flowering worlds, their leaves full-grown.

As into some unheard-of dogma
I move across into this night,
Where a worn poplar age has grizzled
Screens the moon's strip of fallow light,

Where the pond lies, an open secret,
Where apple bloom is surf and sigh,
And where the garden, a lake dwelling,
Holds out in front of it the sky.

THE URALS FOR THE FIRST TIME

Without an accoucheuse, in darkness, pushing her
Blind hands against the night, the Ural fastness, torn and
Half-dead with agony, was screaming in a blur
Of mindless pain, as she was giving birth to morning.

And brushed by chance, tall ranges far and wide
Loosed toppling bronze pell-mell in thunder-colored rumbling.
The train panted and coughed, clutching the mountainside,
And at that sound the ghosts of fir trees shied and stumbled.

The smoky dawn was a narcotic for the peaks,
A drug with which the fire-breathing dragon plied them,

As when a specious thief upon a journey seeks
To lull his fellow travelers with opium slipped them slyly.

They woke on fire. The skies were poppy-colored flame,
Whence Asiatics skied like hunters after quarry;
To kiss the forests' feet the eager strangers came
And thrust upon the firs the regal crowns they carried.

Arrayed in majesty, by rank the firs arose,
Those shaggy dynasts, their grave glory clamant,
And trod the orange velvet of the frozen snows
Spread on a tinseled cloth and richly damasked.

SPRING

How many buds, how many sticky butts
Of candles, April kindled, now are glued
Fast to the boughs! The park is redolent
Of puberty. The woods' retorts are rude.

The forest's throat is caught in a thick knot
Of feathered throats: a lassoed buffalo
Bellowing in the nets as organs pant:
Wrestlers who groan sonatas, deep and slow.

Oh, poetry, be a Greek sponge supplied
With suction pads, a thing that soaks and cleaves,
For I would lay you on the wet green bench
Out in the garden, among sticky leaves.

Grow sumptuous frills, fabulous hoopskirts, swell,
And suck in clouds, roulades, ravines, until
Night comes; then, poetry, I'll squeeze you out
And let the thirsty paper drink its fill.

THREE VARIATIONS

1.

When consummate the day hangs before you,
Each detail to be scanned at your ease,
Just the sultry chatter of squirrels
Resounds in the resinous trees.

And storing up strength in their languor,
The ranked piney heights are adrowse,
While the freckled sweat is pouring
From the peeling forest's boughs.

2.

Miles thick with torpor nauseate the gardens.
The catalepsy of the valleys' rage
Is weightier, more threatening than a tempest,
Fiercer than hurricane's most savage raid.

The storm is near. The dry mouth of the garden
Gives off the smell of nettles, roofs, and fear,
And of corruption; and the cattle's bellow
Rises columnar in the static air.

3.

Now tatters of denuded clouds
Grow on each bush in tasseled groves.
Damp nettles fill the garden's mouth.
It smells of storms and treasure troves.

The shrubs are tired of lament.
In heaven arched prospects multiply.
Like web-toed birds on swampy ground
The barefoot azure treads the sky.

And willow branches and the leaves
Of oaks, and tracks beside the spring,
Like lips the hand has not wiped dry,
Are glistening, are glistening.

IMPROVISATION

A flock of keys I had feeding out of my hand,
To clapping of wings and croaking and feathery fight;
On tiptoe I stood and stretched out my arm, and the sleeve
Rolled up, so I felt at my elbow the nudging of night.

And the dark. And a pond in the dark, and the lapping of waves.
And the birds of the species I-love-you that others deny
Would be killed, so it seemed, before the savage black beaks,
The strong and the strident, were ever to falter and die.

And a pond. And the dark. And festive the palpitant flares
From pipkins of midnight pitch. And the boat's keel gnawed
By the wave. And always the greedy noise of the birds
Who fighting over the elbow fluttered and cawed.

The gullets of dams were agurgle, gulping the night.
And the mother birds, if the fledgelings on whom they dote
Were not to be fed, would kill, so it seemed, before
The roulades would die in the strident, the crooked throat.

OUT OF SUPERSTITION

The cubbyhole I live in is a box
    Of candied orange peel.
Soiled by hotel rooms till I reach the morgue—
    That's not for me, I feel.

Out of pure superstition I have come
   And settled here once more.
The wallpaper is brown as any oak,
   And there's a singing door.

I kept one hand upon the latch, you tried
   To fight free of the nets,
And forelock touched enchanted forelock, and
   Then lips touched violets.

O softy, in the name of times long gone,
   You play the old encore:
Your costume like a primrose chirps "Hello"
   To April as before.

It's wrong to think—you are no vestal: you
   Brought in a chair one day,
Stood on it, took my life down from the shelf
   And blew the dust away.

"WAVING A BOUGH"

Waving a bough full of fragrance,
In the dark, with pure good to sup,
The water the storm had made giddy
Went running from cup to cup.

From chalice to chalice rolling,
It slid along two and hung,
One drop of agate, within them,
Shining and shy it clung.

Over the meadowsweet blowing,
The wind may torture and tear

At that drop—it will never divide it,
Nor the kissing, the drinking pair.

They laugh and try to shake free and
Stand up, each straight as a dart,
But the drop will not leave the stigmas,
Wild horses won't tear them apart.

"FRESH PAINT"

I should have seen the sign: "Fresh paint,"
   But useless to advise
The careless soul, and memory's stained
   With cheeks, calves, hands, lips, eyes.

More than all failure, all success,
   I loved you, for your skill
In whitening the yellowed world
   As white cosmetics will.

Listen, my dark, my friend: by God,
   All will grow white somehow,
Whiter than madness or lamp shades
   Or bandage on a brow.

DEFINITION OF THE SOUL

To fly off, a ripe pear in a storm,
With one leaf clinging on as it must.
Mad devotion! It quitted the branch!
It will choke with its throat full of dust!

A ripe pear, more aslant than the wind.
What devotion! "You'll bray me? You're brash!"
Look! In beauty the thunder-spent storm
Has blazed out, crumbled down—sunk to ash.

And our birthplace is burned to a crisp.
Say, fledgeling, where now is your nest?
O my leaf, with the fears of a finch!
My shy silk, why still fight and protest?

Rest in concrement, song, unafraid.
Whither now? All striving is naught.
Ah, "here": mortal adverb! The throb
Of concrescence could give it no thought.

RUPTURE

9.

The piano, aquiver, will lick the foam from its lips.
The frenzy will wrench you, fell you, and you, undone,
Will whisper: "Darling!" "No," I shall cry, "what's this?
In the presence of music!" Of nearness there is none

Like twilight's, with the chords tossed into the fireplace
Like fluttering diaries, for one year, and two, and three.
O miraculous obit, beckon, beckon! You may
Well be astonished. For—look—you are free.

I do not hold you. Go, yes, go elsewhere,
Do good. *Werther* cannot be written again,
And in our time death's odor is in the air:
To open a window is to open a vein.

1918

"HERE THE TRACE"

Here the trace of enigma's strange fingernail shows.
"It is late. Let me sleep, and at dawn I'll reread
And then all will be clear. Till they wake me, there's none
Who can move the beloved as I move her, indeed!"

How I moved you! You bent to the brass of my lips
As an audience stirred by a tragedy thrills.
Ah, that kiss was like summer. It lingered, delayed,
Swelling slow to a storm as it topples and spills.

As the birds drink, I drank. Till I swooned, still I sucked.
As they flow through the gullet, the stars seem to stop.
But the nightingales shuddering roll their bright eyes,
As they drain the vast vault of the night, drop by drop.

1918

SPRING

I've come from the street, Spring, where the poplar stands
Amazed, where distance quails, and the house fears it will fall,
Where the air is blue, like the bundle of wash in the hands
Of the convalescent leaving the hospital;

Where evening is empty: a tale begun by a star
And interrupted, to the confusion of rank
On rank of clamorous eyes, waiting for what they are
Never to know, their bottomless gaze blank.

1918

"WE'RE FEW"

We're few, perhaps three, hellish fellows
Who hail from the flaming Donetz,

219

With a fluid gray bark for our cover
Made of rain clouds and soldiers' soviets
And verses and endless debates
About art or it may be freight rates.

We used to be people. We're epochs.
Pell-mell we rush caravanwise
As the tundra to groans of the tender
And tension of pistons and ties.
Together we'll rip through your prose,
We'll whirl, a tornado of crows,

And be off! But you'll not understand it
Till late. So the wind in the dawn
Hits the thatch on the roof—for a moment—
But puts immortality on
At trees' stormy sessions, in speech
Of boughs the roof's shingles can't reach.

1921

"YOU PICTURES FLYING"

You pictures flying slantwise in a shower
From the highway that blew the candle out,
I can't teach you to keep from rhyme and measure,
Deserting hooks and walls in your skew rout.

Suppose the universe goes masked? Or even
That every latitude breeds some of those
Who are on hand to stop its mouth with putty
And seal it for the winter: just suppose!

Yet objects tear their masks off, all their power
Leaks out, they leave their honor where it lies,
Should there be any reason for their singing,
Should the occasion for a shower arise.

1922

ROOSTERS

Nightlong the water labored breathlessly.
Till morning came, the rain burned linseed oil.
Now vapor from beneath the lilac lid
Pours forth: earth steams like *shchee* * that's near the boil.

And when the grass, shaking itself, leaps up,
Oh, who will tell the dew how scared I am—
The moment the first cock begins to yawp,
And then one more, and then—the lot of them?

They name the years as these roll by in turn,
And on each darkness, as it goes, they call,
Foretelling thus the change that is to come
To rain, to earth, to love—to each and all.

1923

TO A FRIEND

Come, don't I know that, stumbling against shadows,
Darkness could never have arrived at light?
Do I rate happy hundreds over millions
Of happy men? Am I a monster quite?

Isn't the Five-Year Plan a yardstick for me,
Its rise and fall my own? But I don't quiz
In asking: What shall I do with my thorax
And with what's slower than inertia is?

The great Soviet gives to the highest passions
In these brave days each one its rightful place,
Yet vainly leaves one vacant for the poet.
When that's not empty, look for danger's face.

* *Cabbage soup.*

221

LYUBKA

Not long ago the rain walked through this clearing
Like a surveyor. Now with tinsel bait
The lily of the valley's leaves are weighted,
And water got into the mullein's ears.

These are the frigid fir trees' quondam nurslings,
Their ear lobes stretched with dew; they shun the day,
And grow apart, single and solitary,
Even their odors separately disbursed.

When it is teatime in the summer villas,
The fog fills the mosquito's sail, and night,
Plucking the strings of a guitar but lightly,
Stands among pansies in a mistlike milk.

Then with nocturnal violet all is scented.
Faces and years. And thoughts. Every event
That from the thievish past can be commanded
And in the future taken from Fate's hand.

1927

From WAVES

I

We were in Georgia. You can get this land
If hell is multiplied by paradise,
Bare indigence by tenderness, and if
A hothouse serves as pedestal for ice.

And then you'll know what subtle doses of
Success and labor, duty, mountain air
Make the right mixture with the earth and sky
For man to be the way we found him there.

So that he grew, in famine and defeat
And bondage, to this stature, without fault,
Becoming thus a model and a mold,
Something as stable and as plain as salt.

II

The Caucasus lay spread before our gaze,
An unmade bed, it seemed, with tousled sheets;
The blue ice of the peaks more fathomless
Than the warmed chasms with their harbored heats.

Massed in the mist and out of sorts, it reared
The steady malice of its icy crests
As regularly as the salvos spat
In an engagement from machine-gun nests.

And staring at this beauty with the eyes
Of the brigades whose task it was to seize
The region, how I envied those who had
Palpable obstacles to face like these.

O if we had their luck! If, out of time,
As though it peered through fog, this day of ours,
Our program, were of such substantial stuff,
And frowned down at us as this rough steep lours!

Then day and night our program would march on,
Setting its heel upon my prophecies,
Kneading their downpour with the very sole
Of its straight backbone into verities.

There would be no one I could quarrel with,
And not another hour would I give
To making verses: unbeknown to all,
No poet's life, but poems I would live.

1931

"IF ONLY, WHEN I MADE MY DEBUT"

If only, when I made by debut,
There might have been a way to tell
That lines with blood in them can murder,
That they can flood the throat and kill,

I certainly would have rejected
A jest on such a sour note,
So bashful was that early interest,
The start was something so remote.

But age is pagan Rome, demanding
No balderdash, no measured breath,
No fine feigned parody of dying,
But really being done to death.

A line that feeling sternly dictates
Sends on the stage a slave, and, faith,
It is good-by to art forever
Then, then things smack of soil and Fate.

Ilya Ehrenburg

"THE SONS OF OUR SONS"

The songs of our sons will marvel,
Paging the textbook:
"1914 . . . 1917 . . . 1919 . . .
How did they live? The poor devils!"
Children of a new age will read of battles,
Will learn the names of orators and generals,
The numbers of the killed,
And the dates.
They will not know how sweetly roses smelled above the trenches,
How martins chirped blithely between the cannon salvos,
How beautiful in those years was
Life.
Never, never did the sun laugh so brightly
As above a sacked town,
When people, crawling out of their cellars,
Wondered: is there still a sun?
Violent speeches thundered,
Strong armies perished,
But the soldiers learned what the scent of snowdrops is like
An hour before the attack.
People were led at dawn to be shot . . .
But they alone learned what an April morning can be.
The cupolas gleamed in the slanting rays,
And the wind pleaded: Wait! A minute! Another minute!
Kissing, they could not tear themselves from the mournful mouth,
And they could not unclasp the hands so tightly joined.
Love meant: I shall die! I shall die!
Love meant: Burn, fire, in the wind!
Love meant: O where are you, where?
They love as people can love only here, upon this rebellious and
    tender star.

In those years there were no orchards golden with fruit,
But only fleeting bloom, only a doomed May.
In those years there was no calling: "So long!"
But only a brief, reverberant "Farewell!"
Read about us and marvel!
You did not live in our time—be sorry!
We were guests of the earth for one evening only.
We loved, we destroyed, we lived—in the hour of our death.
But overhead stood the eternal stars,
And under them we begot you.
In your eyes our longing still burns,
In your words our revolt reverberates yet.
Far into the night, and into the ages, the ages, we have scattered
The sparks of our extinguished life.

1919

TO RUSSIA

You reek, swollen with hunger, blood and pus ooze from your open
    wounds.
Clinging to mother earth, you writhe and scream.
Your birth throes they mistook, oh, Russia, for your agony,
They're spurning you, the clever ones, the well fed and the clean.
Their wombs are barren, slack breasts turned to stone.
What rightful heir awaits the ancient heritage?
Who now will kindle and bear forth
Prometheus' half-quenched flame?
The hour is grave and dire, the event austere.
Upon a dunghill wet with our hot blood,
Not from the air, nor from the blue sea's foam
A great new age is born.
Have faith in it! Receive it from our hands!
Both ours and yours, it will efface all boundaries.
Forgotten, in the northern capital
Beneath a shroud of snows life barely breathed.

Sometimes a people will be summoned for a space
To water with its blood the furrowed earth: by every road
Your persecutors, motherland, will come to you,
Kissing your bloody footprints on the snow.

1920

"BUT TELL ME"

But tell me, was there life here, too,
And houses in a blaze of green?
The sky, the ashes, like the caps
Worn by the shot, afford no clue.

Alone the hanged looks grim; as though
He were a solemn pendulum,
He keeps on swinging back and forth
Counting the hours as they go.

1944

THE TREE

The meek dew shone, the grass lay prostrate
As humbly as a slave will lie,
And veering from the roof the swallow
Had sought the wide and tender sky.

And you alone, great tree, remaining
There at your post, stood straight and still,
Lonely and stubborn as a soldier
Whose duty was to hold the hill.

And under fire you tossed and twisted,
As through your boughs the torment ran,
And when you met your mortal moment
You died as gravely as a man.

1945

Marina Tzvetayeva

"NO LONGER NOW"

No longer now the same god-given bounties
Where now no longer the same waters glide.
Then fly, and hasten, doves of Aphrodite,
Through the great gates that sunset has swung wide.

And I on the chill sands shall lie, receding
Into the dimness of unreckoned days . . .
Like the shed skin the snake is coldly eyeing,
My youth, outgrown, has shrunk under my gaze.

1921

Eduard Bagritzky

"MY HONEYED LANGUOR"

My honeyed languor comes
                    of silence and of dreams
And boredom long-drawn-out
                    and songs that gauchely yearn;
The cocks embroidered on white towels give me joy,
I like the soot that clings to icons old and stern.

To the hot buzz of flies
                    day after day goes by,
And a meek piety on each its blessing lays;
Beneath low ceilings quails
                    are mumbling sleepily;
The smell of raspberry jam pervades the holidays.

At night the billowing
                    soft goose down wearies me,
The stuffy icon lamp blinking is sad to view,
And as he cranes his neck
                    the gay embroidered bird
Commences his long chant
                    of cock-a-doodle-doo.

Here you have granted me
                    a modest refuge, Lord,
Beneath a blissful roof
                    where turmoil cannot grow,
Where clotted days like jam
                    that from a teaspoon drips
In heavy drops
            perpetually flow, flow, flow.

1919

"BLACK BREAD"

Black bread and a faithful wife
Have made us anemic, undone us for life. . . .

Our years have been tested by hoof and by stone,
The waters we drink of with wormwood are strewn,
The taste of the wormwood is stinging our lips. . . .
The knife does not fit the grip of our fists,
The pen does not suit us, but we have grown
Too proud for the pickax, and yet for us
Glory no longer is glorious:
We're the rusty leaves
Upon rusty oaks . . .
When the wind blows,
When the cold grows,
We fall in droves.
On whose path are we spread?
Whose feet will yet tread
The carpet our thick rust weaves?
Will the young trumpeters trample us? Will
Strange constellations rise in our skies?
We're the last warmth nestling in rusty oaks. . . .
We drive the warmth off in our homeless chill. . . .
We fly off into the night!
We fly off into the night!
We fly like ripe stars, as blind in our flight.
Over us the young trumpeters tramp,
Over us strange constellations rise,
Over us whip the flags of an unknown camp . .
When the wind blows,
When the cold grows,
Fly after them,
Fling after them,
Over the meadows roll along,
On the steppes break into song!

Trailing the bayonets where through the clouds they gleam,
Trailing the hoofbeat where the forest shadows teem,
Trailing the call of the trumpet drowned in the forest's dream.

1926

SPRING, THE VET, AND I

The sign says HOSPITAL—a blue haze wraps it now.
The veterinary goes over a cow.

The hand painted with manganese
Feels first the udders, then the strong butt of
The tail, and soon the cow
Beneath the bull will stretch and howl with love.
They clear the nuptial circle with their spades,
The starling sings the epithalamy.
The zodiac has come to earth: Pisces
Is in the pond, and in the grass Taurus is plain to see.

> (The world of wet boughs swells
> To fill the sky.
> The orange wasp casts spells
> In the wet arbors. Why,
> Even the caged larks try
> Their voices: there's so much to tell!)

The sign says HOSPITAL; above, blue haze expands.
With quiet zest the vet washes his hands.

A noise behind the gates.
Let's see what's doing.
Swelling their flanks, the cows
Drift dimly, mooing;
Like spotted smoke they move,

231

Misty with milk and grassy memories
Of meadow haze. Dew hangs like bells
Upon their horns. Blue vapor seethes
About those steady feet.
Well, vet, what are you thinking of?
Now it is time for you to lay your hands
Upon these beasts: to bless alike repose and movement and
Death, and the aching howl of love.

(The household of the April world:
The bugs and lizards, tiny things,
Parcel this earth among them, take
And split it into bits:
Ah, boys on swings,
How the boughs shake!)

The sign says HOSPITAL—a blue haze wraps it yet.
I'm here! I'm near! Old vet!

I stand above you like your conscience, vet.
I make the rounds of all your days like death!
Don't stop!
Work till you drop!
Fight with your wife!
Get drunk!
But keep your faith with life! Don't fail!
Into the crock of milk a warm star falls.
The world lies seamless,
Ironed-out and clean.
It bursts with green,
It shines like water,
Like a maple leaf
Washed by the rain!
It's close! It flutters at your elbow! Seize it and
Squeeze it like a quick bird in your hand!

(A star stands on the door sill—
Do not scare it!
Woods, roads, ravines—
Oh, life unplumbed!
A star stands on the sill—
Don't scare it now, keep still!)

Above the sign blue haze coils lazily.
Off in the distance the vet bows to me.

Upon his perch the starling tries his best.
Earth steams as though fresh from a Turkish bath. No wind.
Above the birds in space that's thinned
To emptiness the planets knock
One on another with a cobbled sound.
Wild geese have a date
With rivery countries.
And the attendants make
For town, with huge stars tête-à-tête.
Earth flows with semen.

(Child of labor, rise,
Barefooted, stirred;
This world is yours to seize
As though it were a honeycomb
Sparkling with dew for you!
Oh, whirl of vernal suns,
Young surf of seas!)

1930

Nikolay Tikhonov

"FIRE, THE ROPE"

Fire, the rope, the bullet and the ax,
Like servants bowed and followed where we went,
And in each drop that fell a deluge slept,
Pebbles grew into mountains where they lay,
And in a small twig trodden underfoot
Whole forests rustled, their black arms outspread.

At table falsehood ate and drank with us,
Bells tolled out of mere habit stupidly,
Our coins lost weight and rang a thinner chime,
And children looked on corpses without fear.
Those were the days when first it was we learned
Words bitter, beautiful and harsh.

1921

"OUR ROOMS"

Our rooms are turned to rolling wagons
With wheels that creak on roads of air;
And down below, the moony water
Is playing gently with green hair.

We travel over crystal bridges,
Across the earth, across the sky.
Its red cheek pressed against our windows,
The sun sings out as we roll by.

And every heart's a summer beehive
Blazing with a dark honeyed gleam,

As though we were the lucky first ones
To bend our heads above the stream.

We do not know who leads us onward,
What end our hurrying wheels will find,
But, like a bird set free, the spirit
Darts on a wing that rips the wind.

1921

"WE HAVE UNLEARNED"

We have unlearned how to give alms, forgotten
How to breathe the salt air above the sea,
And how to meet the dawn, and in the market
Buy golden lemons for two coins or three.
Ships call on us only by chance, and freight trains
Bring cargoes out of habit, that is all;
Just count the men belonging to my country—
How many dead will answer to the call!
But we have no occasion to be solemn—
A broken knife's no good to work with, but
With the same knife that is all black and broken
Know that immortal pages have been cut.

1922

Pavel Antokolsky

HATE!

Hate, be a faithful prop, and find
The words most biting and most fit,
So that filth brings no vertigo
To him who bends so close to it;

So that the honest artist spurns
The facile phrase, the weak excuse,
And is the first one to detect
The coward's lie, the traitor's truce;

So that the artist may be schooled
In probing, judging, and may sense
Just what a deposition means
And learn the tongue of evidence;

So that he trains his eye to catch
A wolfish trick, and warns us all
If silently the enemy
Slips past, or waits and hugs the wall,

Or if, again, with zealous mien
And upraised fist the foe votes "Aye,"
Not caught red-handed yet, not known
And named as one who lives a lie;

Until our enemy must run
From verse as one who on the stair
Hears the police, then drops in dread
And cannot cover his despair.

1938

Nikolay Kluyev

"ON THE FIRS"

On the firs the sunset dozes;
Brown the field, the hedge is green;
Mossy clefts worn rock discloses
Hold spring moisture, meek and clean.

Oh, my woods, these pulses leap
Seeing you so lush and calm!
Piously wild berries weep,
Listening to the grassy psalm.

And I feel no fleshly tie;
Now my heart's a springing mead.
Come, you white-winged birds and shy,..
Peck the early wheaten seed.

Tender evening twilight searches
Cottage windows, gabled byres,
And the leaves of slender birches
Glimmer soft as wedding fires.

1919

A COTTAGE SONG

The stove is orphaned now; the old housewife has died,
The trivet tells the pot with tears; their talk is harried.
Behind the pane two trustful magpies, side by side,
Chirp: "May is near, today the finches will be married,
Smith Woodpecker with busy knocking has stripped his throat,
The mole—that sullen miner—creeps sunward, meekly leaving
His tunneled dark estate to bugs without a groat;

The cranes are homing now, the sparrow, pert and thieving,
Has heard the jackdaw blurt the secret of her egg."
The tangled mop awaits the bucket, limp and tired;
She thinks the unwashed porch for spuming suds must beg.
How gay would be the splash of water, how desired
A window full of sunray tow, an endless fairy tale. . . .
Behind the stove the house sprite gabbles, quick and clever,
Of the new tenant's stillness within the churchyard's pale,
Of crosses listening to things nameless forever,
Of how the dark church entry lulls the lingering dream.
The house sprite gabbles on above the bleak hour's starkness.
The peasant hut is scowling; a pewter eye agleam,
The lonely window stares out at the thaw and darkness.

1920

Pyotr Oreshin

NOT BY HANDS CREATED

1.

Fall on your face,
Flop
Mug-forward into the swamps.
With your old werewolf's eye,
Cataract-blinded,
See
What a buck I am!

2.

Carrot-haired
Big-headed dawns,
And
The darkness of forests,
Rye,
And
The sheaves beyond the village—
My body.

3.

Ears:
Burdocks of cloud,
Long ones, tufted
With red hairs,
Flap
Like asses' ears
Against the sky.

4.

Two
Convulsed eyes—

Two
Oceans resting in me,
And
Thick bulbous lashes
Burn green
On my cheekbones!

5.

My stone
Mouth
Is stretched
With song
From east to west.
And

6.

Legs
And hoofs
Kicked skyward
And
The claw
On my hairy
Paw
Blazes!

7.

Gorged
And motionless,
Like a bull,
I have squatted, rocklike,
In a long shirt
Of sunsets,
And I sit
Sprawled out
On the fat mound of the Universe.

8.

Dark forests
Grow
Out of
My hairy belly.
In the stone
Fir trees
Gray wolves,
In cope and coif,
Having lit tapers,
Serve mass.

9.

Eternal,
Not-by-hands-created,
I roll my eyes
Heavily
Like
The millstones
Of blue
Heavenly mills!

10.

Slowly
I chew the cud of gray clouds,
And
Think of
Perishing brothers
With my wise
Cheerful belly!

11.

Through closed lids
I see:
Between my legs
New rivers

Rock
A new firmament
Upon golden crests.

12.

Listening to the World,
I spit
With lower lip
Out-thrust,
And lo!
Rains
Pour
Like spears
And
Clinking
Stick in the earth.

13.

Eternal,
Not-by-hands-created,
The spirit
Of life-giving spring
I waft
Over the tilled field,
And
On the naked knees of the Universe
I pour
The blue semen
Of my eternal triumph.
Hosanna in the highest!

1918

THE TAILOR

I'm sharp as a needle today,
I worked till the last light had fled,

Till night raised her long blue-black sleeve
To pour all her stars on my head.

I got a big order today:
To sew men together, as one,
And it's glad of my needle I am,
And it's soon that the job should be done.

Come to me, you with souls full of holes,
I'll mend and darn fine as you please.
Beat, red heart, in my breast!
Let me drain my dream to the lees!

Here in Shop Twenty-One
Over his work each leans
With joy, for he hears as one
The hum of our fiery machines.

Thriddle-thrum, thriddle-thrum-thrum!
The shuttle moves fast, like a heart,
The red thread gleams like a dream,
Our strength is our best head start.

We're tailors of golden worlds.
East to West we'll joyfully sew.
We'll shelter in tents of the sun,
Where the red world spins, we'll go.

Thriddle-thrum, shuttle, be quick!
Bright needle, stitch firmly each hour!
We must finish on time, that life
May be a red garden in flower.

Sergey Yesenin

"WHERE DAWN IS SPRINKLING"

Where dawn is sprinkling her red waters on
The cabbages and beets,
A little nuzzling maple reaches up
To suck its dam's green teats.

1910

AUTUMN

How still it is among the junipers!
Autumn—a bay mare—cleans her mane of burrs.

Her hoofs' blue clatter sounds above the bank
Of the still river where the reeds are rank.

The monkish wind steps gingerly, his tread
Kneads the heaped leaves with which the road is spread,

And at the rowan clusters he will lean
To kiss the red wounds of the Christ unseen.

1914

"IN THE CLEAR COLD"

In the clear cold the dales grow blue and tremble;
The iron hoofs beat sharply, knock on knock.
The faded grasses in wide skirts assemble
Flung copper where the wind-blown willows rock.

From empty glens, a slender arch ascending,
Fog curls upon the air and mosswise grows,
While evening, low above the river bending,
In its white waters washes his blue toes.

1915

DROVES

Upon green hills in droves the horses graze
And blow the golden bloom off passing days.

From the high slope into the azure bay
Tumbles the pitch of heavy manes asway.

They toss their heads above the still lagoon,
Caught with a silver bridle by the moon.

Snorting in fear of their own shadows, they,
Whose manes will screen it, wait the coming day.

1915

"HOPES, PAINTED"

Hopes, painted by the autumn cold, are shining;
My steady horse plods on as calm as Fate;
His dun lip twitches moistly at the lining
Of my blown coat; he does not change his gait.

On a far road the unseen traces, leading
Neither to rest nor battle, lure and fade;
The golden heels of day will flash, receding,
And labors in the chest of years be laid.

1915

TRANSFIGURATION

III.

Ho, Russians,
Fishers of the universe,
You who scooped heaven with the net of dawn,
Blow your trumpets!

Beneath the plow of storm
The earth roars.
Golden-tusked, the colter breaks
The cliffs.

A new sower roams the fields;
New seeds
He casts into the furrows.

A radiant guest drives toward you
In a coach.
Across the clouds
A mare races.

The breeching on the mare:
The blue;
The bells on the breeching:
The stars.

1918

THE JORDAN DOVE

2.

The moon is the tongue
In the bell of the sky;
My country's my mother,
A Bolshevik, I.

That all may be brothers
Is cause for me
To rejoice in your death,
My own country.

Sturdily, loudly
I ring the blue bell,
And make the moon swing for
Your passing knell.

Yours, world of brothers,
The song I raise.
I hear glad tidings
Float through the haze.

1918

"OH, LISTEN"

Oh, listen—the sleigh's rushing on, the sleigh's rushing on, do you
    hear?
It is good to be lost in the hushed snowy fields with my dear.

The gay wind is bashful—advancing and shyly retreating again.
And a bell goes on rolling and rolling across the bare plain.

Then it's hey, my sleigh! Hey, my sleigh! Yes, and it's ho, my dun
    horse in the snows!
In a clearing a drunken young maple twirls round on her toes.

We will drive up and ask: What's the matter? And then in a twink
    there will be
An accordion playing, and we'll dance together all three.

1925

247

"A MOONY THIN DESOLATION"

A moony thin desolation,
Vast plains in anguish immersed—
My carefree youth once knew this,
I loved it, like others, and cursed.

The roads with their dusty willows,
And the tune that the cartwheels play . . .
Not for aught that I might be offered
Would I listen to it today.

I am weary of huts and hearthstones,
Spring storming the apple trees
I can love no longer for thinking
Of the fields in their poverty.

Now my heart is given elsewhere—
In the moon's consumptive light
I see stone and steel as the secret
Of my country's coming might.

Oh, Russia, give over dragging
Your wooden plow through the fields!
The birches ache, and the poplars,
When they see what the harvest yields.

Perhaps the new life will reject me,
My future is blank, but I feel
A longing to see beggared Russia
Become a Russia of steel.

And hearing the bark of the motors
Where the gusty blizzards throng,
I have no wish at all to listen
To the cartwheels' creaking song.

1925

Anatoly Marienhof

"SAVAGE NOMAD HORDES"

Savage nomad hordes
Of Asia
Spilled fire out of the tubs!
Razin's execution is avenged,
And the piece of Pugachov's * beard
Torn out by the roots.
Hoofs
Have trampled
The scruff of the earth,
Chill with centuries,
And the angelic sky, like a stocking
With a hole in its heel,
Has been taken out of the laundry trough
Clean as clean can be.

1918(?)

* Stepan (Stenka) Razin, celebrated in folk balladry, led a popular rising
in southeastern Russia in 1670–1. Yemelyan Pugachov, a pretender to
the Russian throne, headed a similar rebellion of malcontents a century
later in the reign of Catherine II.

OCTOBER *

We trample filial obedience,
We have gone and sat down saucily,
Keeping our hats on,
Crossing our legs.

You don't like it that we guffaw with blood,
That we don't wash rags washed millions of times,

* The month of the Bolshevik Revolution.

That we suddenly dared
Earsplittingly to bark: Wow!

Yes, sir, the spine
Is as straight as a telephone pole,
Not mine only, but the spines of all Russians,
For centuries hunched.

Who on earth is noisier now than we?
You say: Bedlam—
No mileposts—no landmarks—
Straight to the devil: on the church porch our red cancan is glorious.

You don't believe? Here are hordes,
Droves of clouds at men's beck and call,
And the sky like an old wife's cloak,
And the sun has no eyelashes. . . .

Jesus is on the cross again, and Barabbas
We escort, arm in arm, down Tverskoy Boulevard . . .
Who will break in, who? The gallop of Scythian horses?
Violins bowing the Marseillaise?

Has it ever before been heard of, that the forger
Of rails braceleting the globe
Should smoke his cheap tobacco as importantly
As the officer used to clink his spurs?

You ask: and then?
And then dancing centuries.
We shall knock at all doors
And no one will say: Goddamyou, get out!

We! We! We are everywhere:
Before the footlights, on the proscenium,

250

Not gentle lyricists,
But flaming buffoons.

Pile rubbish, all the rubbish in a heap,
And like Savonarola, to the sound of hymns,
Hurl it into the fire. . . . Whom should we fear?
When the mundiculi of puny souls have become—worlds.

Each day of ours is a new chapter of the Bible.
Every page will be Great to thousands of generations.
We are those about whom they will say:
The lucky ones lived in 1917!
And you still shout: They are lost!

You are still whimpering lavishly!
Dunderheads,
Isn't yesterday crushed, like a dove
By a motor
Dashing madly from the garage?

1918(?)

Alexey Gastev

WE GROW OUT OF IRON

Look! I stand among workbenches, hammers, furnaces, forges, and
  among a hundred comrades.
Overhead hammered iron space.
On either side—beams and girders.
They rise to a height of seventy feet.
They arch right and left.
Joined by cross-beams in the cupolas, with giant shoulders they sup-
  port the whole iron structure.
They thrust upward, they are bold, they are strong.
They demand yet greater strength.
I look at them and grow straight.
Fresh iron blood pours into my veins.
I have grown taller.
I too am growing shoulders of steel and arms immeasurably strong.
I am one with the building's iron.
I have risen.
My shoulders are forcing the rafters, the upper beams, the roof.
My feet remain on the ground, but my head is above the building.
I choke with the inhuman effort, but already I am shouting:
"May I have the floor, comrades, may I have the floor?"
An iron echo drowns my words, the whole structure shakes with
  impatience. And I have risen yet higher, I am on a level with
  the chimneys.
I shall not tell a story or make a speech, I will only shout my iron
  word:
"Victory shall be ours!"

1918

FACTORY WHISTLES

When the morning whistles blow in the factory districts, this is no
    call to slavery. It is the song of the future.
Once upon a time we toiled in humble shops and started work in the
    morning at different hours.
Now the whistles shrill at eight o'clock for a whole million
Now we all start in at once to the minute.
A million men take up the hammers at the same moment.
Our first blows thunder together.
What do the whistles sing about?
They are the morning hymn of unity.

1918

Demyan Bednyi

THE YOUNG FOREST

A landowner, some years ago,
Went driving through his woods, which made a splendid show.
    His coachman, Filka, on his perch
    Looked strong of sinew and of bone.
The landowner admired the woods he called his own.
"Just see my saplings, Filka: pine and birch!
My boy, this is a forest, eh? Look round a bit:
This used to be a waste, but now just look at it!
That's where good switches grow—hop down and fetch a few;
The peasants need their drubbings—rods will come in pat."
"Mm, yes," drawled Filka, "yes . . . the very thing for that . . .
Just let them grow . . . they'll make stout clubs, I promise you."
    The moral of this tale is clear to any cub:
    Years passed, and every switch became a club.

1915

NEPMAN *

Just watch them, comrade . . . with an owner's eye . . .
    And let them pasture on the busy street,
These cattle; let them batten and feed high,
    And so make rich and juicy meat.
Let their fleece grow. But do not let your wits
    Go gathering wool, or they'll give you the slip.
And threaten, not with knives, just with a whip.
    And when the time is ripe, then we'll be quits,
And the whole flock's thick pelts be ours to clip.

1922

* *A private entrepreneur permitted to engage in business under the New Economic Policy inaugurated in 1921.*

NO ONE KNEW

(April 22, 1870)

It was a day like any other,
The same dull sky, the same drab street.
There was the usual angry pother
From the policeman on his beat.
Proud of his fine new miter's luster,
The archpriest strutted down the nave;
And the pub rocked with brawl and bluster,
Where scamps gulped down what fortune gave.
The market women buzzed and bickered
Like flies above the honeypots.
The burghers' wives bustled and dickered,
Eyeing the drapers' latest lots.
An awe-struck peasant stared and stuttered,
Regarding an official door
Where yellow rags of paper fluttered:
A dead ukase of months before.
The fireman ranged his tower, surveying
The roofs, like the chained bears one sees;
And soldiers shouldered arms, obeying
The drill sergeant's obscenities.
Slow carts in caravans went winding
Dockward, where floury stevedores moiled;
And, under convoy, in the blinding
Dust of the road, a student toiled,
And won some pity, thus forlorn,
From the drunk hand who poured his scorn
In curses on some pal and brother. . . .
Russia was aching with the thorn
And bearing her old cross, poor mother,
That day, a day like any other,
And not a soul knew that—*Lenin was born!*

1927

Mikhail Gerasimov

From **THE ELECTRIC POEM**

The First Bulb Lights Up

From what nebula
What star has rolled
Down into these slimy reeds?
The crowd of peasants sways—
Pressed by electric fingers
Of light that crumple
These men of stone.
Smiles stream forth
Through their straw beards.
They swallow the new light, gulping,
And scoop up handfuls
From the spring of light
Jetting under the hand of man.
The floodgate with a desperate sob
Hides under leaping foam.
On skeletal trees,
On posts, we hang
Nerves of light.
The wooden bones of the village,
Its log ribs,
Are worked by copper muscles.
Hundreds of electric fangs
Sink into *izba* ° hearts,
Into the hearts of peasants.
On the age-old blindness of windows,
Black with *luchina* † soot,
Constellations flare.
New eyes are hatched to seize the world.

1923

° *Peasant cottage.*
† *A strip of wood formerly used by peasants as a candle.*

Nikolay Poletayev

RED SQUARE

The windy toss of blood-red banners
Against blue skies more wan than bright,
The silver glinting of their mottoes
Struck by a slant sun's chilly light;

The measured tread of marchers tramping
In serried ranks, the sternness of
Those pale gray faces, and the roaring
Of iron birds far, far above;

No glorying, no jubilation,
No rapture keyed to laughter here;
Alone cold consciousness of duty,
Iron, immutable, and clear.

1918

Vasily Kazin

THE BRICKLAYER

I wander homeward at evening,
Fatigue is a comrade who sticks;
And my apron sings for the darkness
A strong red song of bricks.

It sings of my ruddy burden
That I carried so high, high
Up to the very housetop,
The roof that they call the sky.

My eyes were a carousel turning,
The wind had a foggy tone,
And morning, too, like a worker,
Carried up a red brick of its own.

I wander homeward at evening,
Fatigue is a comrade who sticks;
And my apron sings for the darkness
A strong red song of bricks.

1920

THE CARPENTER'S PLANE

Smoothly riding,
Bravely gliding,
Like a swan my plane swims by.

Now she hurries
Through the flurries
Of the shavings as they fly.

Sail, unbowed one,
Proud one, proud one,
Though the river road be rough.

Warmth is streaming
Through the creaming
Waves of shavings that you slough.

Now she's sweeping
Past the leaping
Swishing waterfalls with ease—

Ah, my beauty,
Do your duty,
While the foam seethes round my knees.

1922

Alexander Bezymensky

VILLAGE AND FACTORY

Huts that stand like plaited baskets.
Birds. Green forest. Space. And heat.
Cobwebs in the dark soul's corners.
Thought's slow whisper. Peace. Retreat.

Dirt and soot. Thick sweaty odors.
Crisp steel shavings. Whistles. Noise.
Straight bold thinking. Heavy labor.
Life's pulse throbbing like a boy's.

1920

Stepan Shchipachev

ON THE BOULEVARD

Oh, what a night! The hoarfrost flies
From every bough in ashen flecks.
The old man with the telescope
Looks like a parrot in his specs.

The others hurry to get warm,
But he is not as others are.
Immune to cold, he sells the sky
To passers-by: a dime a star.

SUNFLOWER

The sunflower has nowhere
to shelter from the rain—
his feet in mud, the water
between the beds won't drain.

Capped, carroty and freckled,
you see the chap remain
fast in the bed—why should he
run? He likes the rain.

1938

"HERE SORROW HAD NO LIMIT"

Here sorrow had no limit and no bottom,
Here poverty tramped the bleak road alone,
Where clasping to their breasts their unweaned babies,
Polish madonnas stood, carved out of stone.

They stared far off into the country distance
Where the thin soil crumbles as it is plowed,
Stood quietly and stared, the only mothers
Whose eyes the tears of sorrow did not cloud.

1939

DUEL

Chiseled in stone, his image will not fade:
It will endure, the hand with the grenade.

A tank must crush whatever meets its mass,
But let a man spring up—it cannot pass.

A burst of ruddy flame, and the tank roars
As shrouding smoke around it blackly pours.

A Russian youngster, helmeted in gray,
Wipes his wet forehead. That was a hot day!

1942

Alexey Surkov

"WHIPPED ON BY DECEMBER"

Whipped on by December, snow storms ahead.
Out there in the snow a German lies dead.

Above him a Russian mother is bent.
She looks at the body, darkly intent.

Now thickly she speaks, and tugs at her shawl:
"I've nothing to mourn you with, nothing at all,

"My tears were a bitter river: it's dry.
Your knife did its work—my man had to die.

"And there was my son, too, just the one son.
You wolf cub, you killed him; now I have none."

1941

Semyon Kirsanov

THIS WILL PASS

If you had died
a hundred years later,
I should have known the painstaking possibilities of science.
I should have known
that the fantastic surgeon of the future
out of the first willing
girl
could make me a you.

The skin and the voice
having been figured out
with the aid of precision instruments,
the Institute of Similars
would have produced
an absolute you.

At first the memories do not coincide,
but that too the fantastic surgeon of the future
can correct.
The childhood of the deceased
is suggested to her,
and for complete resemblance
a safe little tuberculosis
is planted in her lungs.

I am sure that given
my means,
a willing girl would have been found,
she would have come in a stranger
and gone out an absolute you.

And maybe really
in the fantastic future
not I, but someone else
will marry
an absolute you.

I'm not such an egoist,
as long as it's you.

1940

THIS WILL REMAIN

But look: the water
that she lifted in her palms to wash with
is now
in the curve of a cloud
or in a subterranean stream
or in a blade of grass.

And that earth
she walked on,
who loved the May Day square,
that earth either sparkles in the dew
or is coated with tar
or is in the window box where Aunt Motya grows
geranium and aloe.

And the air
she exhaled
also serves a needy blade of grass
somewhere!

I know—
she is
no more.
But the world has somehow been touched by her?

I kiss the pink ticket
with its emblem,
which admitted you
to the speakers' platform
on our first,
your last
May Day.

1940

THE HEART

For twenty days and twenty nights he lay
Still breathing—how, the doctors could not say.
But close beside the bed his mother sat,
And death could not dispatch him, seeing that.

For twenty days and twenty nights she bent
Her eyes upon him, changelessly intent.
But as the twenty-first day dawned, she dozed,
For half a minute then her eyes were closed.
He, fearful lest she waken from her rest,
Silenced the heartbeat in his laboring breast.

1940

Alexander Tvardovsky

THE STARLING

On the porch a trooper marvels
At a starling: "Take my word,
There is something to that fellow,
Yes, a starling's quite a bird.

"In this scorched and blistered garden
That's attached to our new base,
All day long the chap is busy,
Keeps at work about the place;

"He's rebuilding, he's repairing,
Just as if to signify:
War or no war, still the thing is
To increase and multiply."

1945

Konstantin Simonov

"JUST WAIT FOR ME"

Just wait for me and I'll return.
But wait, oh, wait with all your might . . .
Wait when your heart is saddened by
The pouring rains, the sallow light.
Wait when the wind heaps up the snow,
Wait when the air is dry and hot.
Wait when the rest no longer wait
For those whom they too soon forgot.
Wait when the letters fail to come,
Wait on, through dread and through despair,
When those who wait together end
Their waiting and turn otherwhere.

Just wait for me and I'll return.
And show no kindliness to such
As know by heart that it is time
To cease from grieving overmuch.
Let both my mother and my son
Believe me lost, let friends who tire
Of waiting longer sit them down
Barren of hope beside the fire,
And let them toast my memory
In bitter wine as friends will do.
Wait. While they drink, be waiting still,
Nor lift the glass they pour for you.

Just wait for me and I'll return,
To spite all deaths that men can die.
Let those who gave up waiting say:
"It was his luck"—that is a lie.
It is not theirs to understand

Who gave up waiting, wearily,
How under fire I was safe,
Since, waiting, you protected me.
And none but you and I will know
How I escaped the thrust of fate—
Simply because, better than all
The others, you knew how to wait.

1941

Sergey Ostrovoy

LITTLE BIRCH TREE

It was at sundown that I saw it;
A bomber shadowed it, yet bright
It gleamed beside a half-charred paling:
A single birch tree, slim and white.

No whit the smoke of war had smutched it,
More candid shone the little tree,
There at the edge of silence, stretching
Its boughs towards sunset, silently.

No fire had seared those shining branches;
It shed so blithe a light around,
It seemed to warm the air above it
And spread a radiance on the ground.

Can we forget the hour, when pouring
Forth grace, all in her gift to pour,
The birch bade us farewell, who left her
To journey to the work of war?

1944

Sergey Orlov

PAUSE ON THE MARCH

The blazing sun has made the armor hot,
Thick on our clothes the dust of the campaign.
Oh, to pull off the coveralls, and sink
Into the shady grass, but first it's plain

We've got to check the motor, lift the hatch;
Let her cool down. No matter how we feel,
Sure you and I can stand up to the worst:
We're human beings, but she's only steel.

1944

Mikhail Matusovsky

HAPPINESS

When wisps of smoke from the guns were flying
Between the sky and the shaken land,
And men alone could endure the pounding
That was too much for the stones to stand;

When, swathed in flame and in smoky tatters,
The world careened like a ship in churned
Tempestuous seas; when to live was painful
And only dead men were unconcerned;

When, to the creaking of ice in springtime,
I looked about me, a human speck
Alone there, deep in the snow, preparing
To die—the Germans on my neck;

When gunfire woke me and deathy tremors
Convulsed the forest at night, it brought
No dread, no envy of others' fortunes;
I kept revolving a single thought:

To live, not stealthily, not abjectly,
But swoop, an avalanche as it flies!
The happiness I demand is total,
And not on half will I compromise.

1945

LONG ROADS

It was a German town that we awoke in,
With unfamiliar quiet everywhere.

273

These pyramidal roofs are alien to me,
These mean and narrow streets I cannot bear.

I keep on dreaming that I'm done with dreaming
And that I really wake again in sight
Of my own destined city, of my Moscow,
Airy and buoyant and suffused with light.

What's fame to me, mountains of golden treasure,
Rivers of wine? I'd give it all away
If I could see, spread out before my window,
The Russian spaces on a summer's day;

If I could hear, beyond the homely timbers
That wall my cottage, the wet pine trees sough
When autumn comes to bring us gifts of pasties
Bursting with mushrooms—that would be enough;

Only to stub bare feet on the harsh stubble,
Grow tired with walking, day-long on the go,
And on the road in winter note a fox's
Faint tracks, half blotted by the wind-blown snow;

Only to hear the thin chirp of a cricket
Hidden in a dry rick of dusty hay,
To look into a Russian stream for pebbles
That the clear shallows struck with sun display.

The challenge of the town patrol is sterner.
It rains as always from a sky of lead.
Endless the long, long roads that stretch behind me,
And only alien cities lie ahead.

1945

Yevgeny Dolmatovsky

FROST

I wish you'd write me a letter about the frost
(You can't be warm unless there's a frost, you know),
And about the little birch tree, the bashful one,
White as white can be in its cloak of snow.

Write me about the drifts that are piled up
To a giant's shoulders, and tell me everything
About the blizzards that strike so savagely
And kiss so hotly, every kiss a sting.

Write me how thick the ice is in the stream,
And how it sparkles in moonlight; write me all
About the stove, how it crackles cosily,
And how the cricket chirps in a crack in the wall.

Be good and write me about the fire on the hearth,
All the small homely things beyond belief;
I remember how I would hold my wrist to the flame
And it looked transparent as a maple leaf.

. . . Oh, far and far away is my Russia, dressed
In silver, bridal in her bright array,
Here rains run over the sidewalks slantingly,
Spring-fashion, on a January day.

Don't look for blizzards here, don't hope to see
Fresh fallen snow. There is no winter here,
Where men wear rubbers and not thick felt boots,
And capes not overcoats at the end of the year,

Where they have radiators in every room,
Hot baths at any hour, day and night.
But I am lost with nothing to keep me warm.
Send me a snowstorm and I'll be all right.

1946

Nikolay Novosyolov

A DAISY IN AN ALIEN LAND

Where shelved the lifeless clouds are lying
In moth balls stored away, no doubt,
Immobile elms stand still as sentries
On roadways neatly ironed out.

In round lakes quietly reflected
Villas and flowerbeds you see
As squares and ovals: deft solutions
Of problems in geometry.

Meanwhile, in ignorance of every
True geometric principle,
From a black crack a wild steppe daisy
Has sprouted by some miracle.

She languishes. This air is heavy
And without dews. Her wistful stare
Is eastward. Oh, to breathe this moment
But one mouthful of Russia's air!

1946

E. Serebrovskaya

MINES

An orchard will be planted here, you say,
And deep into the earth your spade is thrust.
But battles were fought here: you cannot trust
This ground, a mine may lurk beneath the clay.

Perhaps the sapper missed a single one;
There lies a stupid end, you understand.
A careless step, a movement of the hand—
A blast: and joys and arguments are done.

But here in the old flat I cannot find
A corner that bears touching: everywhere
Letters, belongings, things they used to wear
Who'll not return. Oh, house that grief has mined!

Dumb objects speak, needing nor words nor wits,
Of the misfortune that is hard to brook.
A movement of the hand, a careless look—
And all at once the heart is blown to bits.

1946

Ludmila Tatyanicheva

"THE SNOWSTORMS SLEEP"

The snowstorms sleep, grown weary of pursuit,
The chase was long and they have had their fill.
You barely touched my mouth as you bent to it,
And when you brushed my hand your palm was chill.
But not for naught the winds sang in the dark:
The storm's white horse will rear to its full height,
And suddenly midnight will strike a spark
From the immobile fir trees' malachite.

1946

Nikolay Rylenkov

"GET UP"

Get up—a kerchief thrown across your shoulders,
Go out into the meadows: overhead,
Above the surging flood of the white buckwheat
See where the sails of a great dawn are spread.

The blame will lie with us and that entirely
If, as we watch it riding there on high,
Happiness, slowing slightly as it nears us,
Under such sails as these should pass us by.

1946

Margarita Aliger

YOUR VICTORY

Epilogue

And lo! it shines upon the cities, spreading
this way and that the light none can gainsay;
foreknown for years, at last now here about us
it sheds its grace: the peaceful, human day.
No cannon smoke will dim its gentle glory,
now no one will be wounded, no one killed;
ah, how the soul rejoices in this knowledge,
the promise of its triumph now fulfilled.
And once more man can hear in the fresh silence
the little sounds that for so long were lost;
now he can smile, and wash his hands serenely
in waters of the rivers he has crossed.
And soldiers now will start upon their journey,
and you will see them going back, back, back,
back to their homes, their homes, leaving behind them
the sunsets clotted with a bloody rack.
And we shall greet them, oh, with what a welcome!
We will spare nothing that can make them gay.
But we will leave the revels to the children,
for children know how to keep holiday.
But when triumphal arches cease to echo
with brazen fanfare, when those thunders dim,
then man must find the courage that is needful
to face the world that has been given him.
It has not yet been mended, it is stricken,
looted, and poor, yet shining here and there
the friendly light of peaceful homely duties
makes human labor excellently fair,
and there is rest, and freedom.

                           But it may be
we should expect another fate than this?
Youth, has not the time come for us to sever?

Good-by—I shall not find you one to miss.
Youth is a time of tumult and of chaos,
the stern demands upon it never cease.
Youth never has a chance; that is my sorrow;
I can't put up with it—leave me in peace!
Youth's importunity is but a burden.
Leave me alone, get out. I've paid my debt.
"It is not time for me to go," Youth answers.
The heart responds insistently, "Not yet."
The heart repeats: "Not yet. Let us consider,
and look into the future once again.
It's not yet time to rest, and you don't wish to.
Don't lie, not to yourself or other men.
You have not traveled through the world, traversing
These years, these sorrows, with a step so bold,
Just to surrender now. It is not time yet.
And don't blame Youth. You never will be old.
Your youth is not your wealth, for your disposal,
nor is it a hard row for you to hoe.
Our feet have made immortal tracks already
on a long road, and we have far to go.
Not all the pathways have been mapped and traveled,
there still are answers that nobody knows.
Festive and sacred the alarm is sounding
and in the silence the clear summons grows.
Then bon voyage!
                    Through bright or stormy weather
fare forward, mindful of past charity
and free of malice.
                    Know, the world is given
to those who cling to youth most greedily.
We are in harness, in the field, attacking.
There's no long furlough till our service ends.
Get ready for the road, my generation!
Fare forward boldly, bon voyage, my friends.

1945

Nikolay Lvov

"I TROD UPON THE AGE'S HEELS"

I trod upon the age's heels, pressed closer
And felt its very breath, but never turned;
Upon its chilly iron I was bedded
And where I walked its scorching fires burned.

We moved together to the bourne of courage,
It holds my eyes, my soul: they'd pay the cost
In blood if I should try to tear them from it
Like hands soldered to iron by the frost.

1947

Biographical Notes

Anna Akhmatova (Anna Andreyevna Gorenko), born in 1888, the daughter of an official in the Navy Department, was educated at an institute for well born maidens and traveled abroad. She married Nikolay Gumilyov, the poet, later divorcing him. The first of her slender volumes of verse was published in 1912, the sixth in 1923. Thereafter she remained virtually silent, continuing to live in Leningrad, and only in 1940 there appeared a selection from all her books and magazine verse. The Revolution did not exile her, though she continued to hold to the ideal of a personal and independent art in defiance of the officially sponsored view. The few poems from her pen which were published during World War II, and some of which voiced a stern patriotism, showed that her delicate and subtle art had undergone no change. During the siege of Leningrad she was evacuated to Tashkent.

On August 14, 1946, the Central Committee of the Communist Party, after hearing a now famous report by its secretary, the late Andrey Zhdanov, passed a resolution stating that Akhmatova's poems "suffused as they are with the spirit of pessimism and decadence," were harmful to the education of the Soviet youth and "could not be tolerated in Soviet literature." Forthwith the writers' organizations passed similar condemnatory resolutions, and the critics hastened to vie with each other in finding her verse tainted with all the deadly sins known to Soviet aesthetics. She was expelled from the Union of Soviet Writers and became a proscribed author, mentioned in print only as a horrible example.

Margarita I. Aliger, apparently a native of the South and an alumna of the Literary Institute of the Union of Soviet Writers, began her career as a writer in 1935, but achieved prominence only with the patriotic verse that she composed during the war. She greeted the coming of peace with a remarkable long autobiographic poem.

Pavel Grigoryevich Antokolsky, born in 1896 in Petersburg into a cultivated and comfortable Jewish family—his father was a lawyer—devoted himself to the theater and to literature. His first book of verse appeared in 1922. In addition to many sophisticated lyrics, he has written a poetic drama and several critical essays. During the recent war he published three collections of verse, including a cycle of poems about his son, who was killed in action.

Eduard Georgievich Bagritzky (Dzyubin), 1895–1934, though the son of a poor Jewish tradesman, received a good general education and studied to be a surveyor. At twenty he broke into print in his native Odessa with some verse. He greeted the Revolution with enthusiasm and, being physically handicapped, fought for it chiefly with his pen. When his first book of verse appeared in 1928, he was already known as a poet and particularly as the author of a long dramatic poem, posing the problem of allegiance to the Soviet regime against the background of the civil war in the South. In the few years that remained to him he brought out two more books of verse, wrote some rhymes for children, recast his dramatic poem as a libretto and started a long narrative piece in his characteristic loose meter. A bedridden invalid, he went on working to the end. His collected poems, published in 1938, show him to have been a conscientious, if uneven, writer possessed of unusual originality and power.

Konstantin Dmitrievich Balmont, 1867–1943, belonged to the landed gentry by birth. He was expelled from the University of Moscow for participation in student disorders, and his first two books of verse, published respectively in 1890 and 1894, were in the tradition of civic poetry. A recrudescence of his youthful political ardor occurred during the upheaval of 1905–1906. But those were just temporary deviations in a poetic career devoted to championing aestheticism, individualism, and the other features of what went by the name of modernism at the turn of the century. He traveled far and wide, his journeys carrying him to Egypt, Mexico, India, the South Seas, and exotic themes abound in his work. His stay abroad was somewhat of an exile, since certain revolutionary poems he had written in 1906 barred him from Russia. Returning home in 1913, he remained there through the First World War and the Revolution, and only in 1920 shook the dust of the Soviet Republic from his feet. He was a prolific poet and a translator from many languages, including English. He gave Russia a complete Shelley and a partial Whitman. The expatriate went on turning out quantities of vacuous verse, not all of which, fortunately, was printed. He died in occupied France after years of insanity, a destitute and forgotten man.

Vasily Vasilyevich Bashkin, 1880–1909, a penniless consumptive youth, wrote stories in the Chekhov manner and, in 1905, brought out a slim book of melancholy poems with muffled overtones of social unrest and revolt.

Demyan Bednyi (Demyan the Poor: Yefim Alexeyevich Pridvorov), 1883–1945, was the son of a railway porter. Wretched as were his early circumstances, he succeeded in getting a university education. He was thirty at the time of the appearance of his first book, a collection of political fables. A few of these had previously been printed in the organ of the Bolshevist faction of the Socialist Party, to which he belonged. When the Bolsheviks came to power, he fought for their cause as a member of the Red Army, but chiefly as a purveyor of numerous propaganda pieces, so that when in 1923 he received the Order of the Red Banner, it was as both soldier and poet of the Revolution. He went on steadily turning out reams of newspaper verse in which he championed the policies of the Soviet government and attacked its enemies. On one occasion, failing to anticipate a twist in the Party line, he fell into official disfavor, but only for a short while. Indeed, he was practically the unacknowledged poet laureate of the regime. His lines mark the common grave of the revolutionary heroes on the Red Square. His work, which often verges on doggerel, is interesting chiefly as an almost day-to-day rhymed commentary on nearly three decades of Soviet history. Its bulk may be judged from the fact that his collected output up to the year 1932 fills nineteen volumes.

Andrey Belyi (Boris Nikolayevich Bugayev), 1880–1934, was reared in an academic atmosphere, his father having been a professor of mathematics at the University of Moscow. There the youth studied the natural sciences, later turning to philosophy and literature. His maiden effort was a piece of rhythmic prose composed in the manner of a symphony. The first volume of his attempts at conventional poetry was published in 1904. Two more books of verse appeared in 1908 and 1909. He also wrote on aesthetics and Russian versification. He lived the double life of an artist and a scholar. A mystic by temperament and conviction, Belyi had for some time been interested in theosophy, and when in 1910 he went abroad, he and his wife became fanatical disciples of Rudolf Steiner, founder of the anthroposophic cult. In 1916 he returned to Russia and two years later, about the time when Blok wrote *The Twelve*—the two men were bound by a stormy friendship—he composed a cycle of poems entitled *Christ Has Risen*, which was interpreted as a hymn to the Revolution. For several years he lived in Germany, continuing to write and publish verse, but the last decade of his life he spent in his native land. Abandoning his anthroposophic faith, he made an unsuccessful effort to adjust himself to the Soviet intellectual climate.

Belyi was not only a poet and critic, but also an experimental novelist of high distinction. In his last years he wrote his memoirs, which are a remarkable historical document. His obituary in *Pravda* declared him to have died "a Soviet author," but his work, unlike Blok's, has not become part of Soviet literature.

Alexander Ilyich Bezymensky, born in 1898, joined the Communist Party shortly after graduation from high school and took part in the revolutionary events of November 1917 in Petrograd. Later he was prominently associated with the Komsomol (League of Communist Youth). In 1920 he brought out his first collection of verse, and he was a charter member of the Moscow group of proletarian writers known as *October*.

"Flesh of the revolution's flesh," as Trotzky called him, he has since written many lyrics and long poems dealing with the Revolution, the Party, and various aspects of Soviet life.

Alexander Alexandrovich Blok, 1880–1921, saw little of his father, who was a professor of law, for immediately after the boy's birth his parents separated. His maternal grandfather was head of the University of Petersburg, and it was in the scholarly and literary atmosphere of that genial academic home that the sensitive boy spent his early years, until his mother, to whom he was deeply devoted, remarried. He began writing verse almost as early as he remembered himself, but his first book of poems did not appear until he was twenty-four. He was then a university student and a married man, his wife being the daughter of the celebrated chemist, Mendeleyev. He followed the events of 1905 with interest, but was not politically-minded, and his contacts were chiefly with fellow poets of the symbolist school, especially Andrey Belyi. As an author of lyrical dramas he also moved in theatrical circles. The circumstances of the married couple, which were at first modest, were soon improved by legacies, and he was able to give himself wholly to literary work. This consisted chiefly of lyrics. He started a semiautobiographical novel in verse, but it remained a fragment.

By the time the First World War broke out, his reputation as one of the foremost poets of his generation was firmly established. He served as a noncombatant, and on the fall of the monarchy was appointed to an investigating commission created by the Provisional government. His political attitude was uncertain, but when the November Revolution occurred it filled him with a kind of mystic joy, although he was not unaware of the tragic implications of the upheaval. In January, 1918, he wrote what is generally considered the outstanding poem of the Revolution: *The Twelve.* In the same month he wrote *The Scythians,* virtually his last poem. Thereafter he did editorial work, made a few public addresses, and composed several essays. He seems to have become disillusioned with the regime that emerged from the Revolution. He died of heart disease in his native Petrograd (Leningrad), as the city was beginning to recover from the ravages of civil war and foreign blockade.

Blok is practically the only symbolist poet whose work is cherished in Soviet Russia. His writings are issued in large popular editions and both his life and works are subjected to painstaking study.

Yevgeny Abramovich Boratynsky, 1800–1844, the scion of an aristocratic family with high court connections, at the age of sixteen was expelled from the Corps of Pages, a very exclusive military school. The disgrace, which brought him to the verge of suicide, may have accentuated his gloomy temper, but the lapse itself was only an aberration in the development of a youth possessed of a singularly keen moral sense. Disbarred from civil service, he entered the army as a private at the age of nineteen. Half a dozen years later he succeeded in obtaining his commission, whereupon he retired and settled in Moscow. The circumstances of his mature life, including his marriage and his contacts with fellow authors, were happy. In 1827 he brought out a book of verse which established his reputation as a thoughtful lyricist of elegiac moods.

Valery Yakovlevich Brusov, 1873–1924, born into a middle-class Moscow family, received a thorough training in the humanities and turned early to literature. In 1894, while still a university student, he contributed a group of poems to a miscellany entitled *Russian Symbolists*. At the same time he brought out a book of translations of Verlaine. The following year his first book of verse appeared with the provocative title, *Chefs-d'œuvre*. Other books followed, some of them under the imprint of a publishing house he had established for the promotion of "the new poetry." By 1904 he was the acknowledged head of the symbolists and editor of their Moscow monthly *Vesy* (The Balance). He was a prolific writer, producing tales, novels, plays, critical essays, literary monographs, in addition to poems, original and translated. His collected works, which began to come out when he was forty, were planned to comprise twenty-five volumes.

After the Revolution Brusov became a member of the Communist Party and held several posts under the Commissariat of Education. Later he joined the faculty of the University of Moscow and founded the Higher Institute of Arts and Letters. He was steadily occupied, lecturing, editing, translating, turning out essays, reviews, studies in metrics. He also wrote a considerable amount of verse, which he tried, unsuccessfully, to make the vehicle of his new political allegiance.

Ivan Alexeyevich Bunin, born in 1870, is a descendant of an old line of nobles that had earlier given Russia the poet Zhukovsky. He spent his boyhood in the feudal atmosphere of a manor, but it was a shabby one. So straitened were the family's circumstances that his schooling was cut short and he had to go to work at an early age. His first book, a collection of poems issued from a provincial press in 1891, passed unnoticed. His short stories attracted more attention, and indeed his wide reputation rests chiefly on his work as a writer of fiction, much of which is available in English translation. Yet not until some twenty years ago did the novelist cease to write distinguished lyrics. He has produced admirable translations of English verse, making real poetry out of Longfellow's *Song of Hiawatha*.

The exotic strain in his poems is due to the fact that he has been something of a wanderer. As soon as his circumstances permitted, he began to travel, particularly in the Near East. He kept aloof from literary cliques, but was generally identified with the group of naturalistic writers headed by Maxim Gorky. Not that he shared the latter's radicalism. In

287

the civil war precipitated by the Revolution, he found himself on the side of the Whites, and in 1920 he expatriated himself, settling in France. He has since maintained an intransigeantly anti-Soviet stand. The emigré's powers as a novelist have been undiminished, but they have been employed to produce nostalgic works about a vanished world. In 1933 Bunin received the Nobel prize, the only Russian author to be so honored.

Georgy Ivanovich Chulkov, 1879–1939, the son of a civil servant, was expelled from medical school as a political offender and deported to Siberia. On his release he settled in Petersburg, established contact with the *avant-garde* poets there and in 1904 published his first book of verse. He continued to write symbolist lyrics, as well as stories, plays, and critical essays, including a piece entitled *On Mystical Anarchism* (1906), which caused a considerable stir. Five years after the Revolution he brought out a book of poems that differed from his earlier work only in having stronger religious overtones. Thereafter he gave up creative writing, confining himself to works of literary scholarship.

Gavriil Romanovich Derzhavin, 1743–1816, born into the lower gentry, was early acquainted with poverty. Though practically a self-taught man, he had a fairly good grounding in the humanities. Despite his contrariness and independence of spirit, he made a brilliant career in an age of favoritism, rising from the lowest rank in the army to the highest posts in the bureaucratic hierarchy under Catherine the Great and her successors. He believed it to be the poet's duty to promote the common good by telling the truth—with a smile—to those in power. His numerous writings, most of them in verse, were the by-product of the busy life of a courtier and high-ranking administrator. Only during his last years, when as a retired statesman he lived in Horatian ease on his estate, was he able to devote himself wholly to literature.

Yevgeny Aronovich Dolmatovsky, born in 1915, an alumnus of the Literary Institute of the Union of Soviet Writers, began publishing in 1933, when he was still a member of the Communist League of Youth. During the late war he brought out two or three collections of verse.

Ilya Grigoryevich Ehrenburg was born in 1891 in Moscow into a wealthy Jewish family, who saw to it that his education included some elements of the Hebraic tradition. In his teens he dabbled in revolutionary propaganda, was expelled from high school, and after getting acquainted with the inside of a prison, at the age of eighteen escaped to Paris. There in 1910 he brought out his first book, a collection of verse. Half a dozen other such collections, some of them under Russian imprints, followed in rapid succession. Meanwhile he had lost his taste for politics. In fact, under the influence of Francis Jammes he was thinking of entering a monastery. Yet when the Russian Revolution occurred he returned home. He stayed there during the first four years of the new regime, seeing it at close range. "A Prayer for Russia" is the title of one of the poems which he composed during that period.

When in 1921 he went back to western Europe, he had little enthusiasm for the Soviet way of life as it was shaping itself. He now devoted himself to writing miscellaneous prose and semijournalistic novels satirizing both capitalism and communism. They won him a reputation which his verse had failed to gain. In the thirties he began to present Soviet life in a more favorable light, so that his work fell in line with Soviet fiction. Early in the recent war he returned to Moscow to become the most prominent and popular Soviet journalist. Simultaneously he resumed writing verse, which, like his dispatches and newspaper articles, centered on the war.

Afanasy Afanasyevich Foeth (Fet), 1820–1892, was brought up as the son of Afanasy Shenshin, a well-to-do landed gentleman. He may actually have been fathered by Johann Foeth, of Darmstadt, to whom the poet's mother, also German, had been married before she threw in her lot with Shenshin and went to live with him in Russia. Her marriage to Shenshin not having been performed by an Orthodox priest, her son was deprived of the right to bear the Shenshin name and to inherit from his "father." The stigma of illegitimacy weighed heavily upon him, and it was only in advanced middle age that he succeeded in removing it by dint of litigation.

Meanwhile he had achieved fame under the name that his mother had once borne. His first book of verse appeared in 1840, but it was the next two volumes, published respectively in 1850 and 1856, that established his reputation as a poet. Then for over a quarter of a century he remained silent. In 1858 he retired from the army and settled down to the life of a gentleman farmer. As the poet of ethereal moods was a practical and tightfisted husbandman, he waxed fat and prosperous with the years. He did not give up his literary friendships with such men as Turgenev and Tolstoy, but unlike them he was a black reactionary, fearful of revolution and believing that art flourished at the foot of the throne.

In his seventh decade the poet came to life again in the sybaritic country gentleman, producing four volumes of verse, appropriately entitled *Evening Fires* (1883–1891). It has been truly said of Foeth that, like the nightingale, he sang only at dawn and at sunset. In his last years he devoted himself to translating the Latin poets.

Alexey Kapitonovich Gastev, born in 1882, had only a trade school education, and worked as a locksmith, when he was not in prison or exile as a political offender. Before the Revolution he published several stories, and in 1918 he brought out a book of poems. It ran through more than one edition, but he gave up writing to devote himself to problems of labor management, as head of the Central Institute of Labor in Moscow.

Mikhail Prokofyevich Gerasimov, born in 1889, was the son of a signalman and an illiterate peasant woman, and had to go to work as a small boy. He attended a trade school and did some studying while serving time for a political offense. In 1907 he emigrated to western Europe, where he worked in factories, tramped, traveled the seas as a stoker. In the First World War he joined the French Army as a volunteer, but was deported to Russia for insubordination and pacifist propaganda. After the Revolution he occupied a variety of responsible posts in Soviet institutions. As a protest against Lenin's New Economic Policy, which he held to be counterrevolutionary, he resigned from the Communist Party. He began to write before 1917, but it was under the new regime that he blossomed out into a prolific "proletarian poet." For the last ten or fifteen years he has not been heard from.

Nikolay Stepanovich Gumilyov, 1886–1921, the son of a navy doctor, studied at the University of Leningrad and at the Sorbonne. In 1910 he married Anna Akhmatova, the poet (from whom he was later divorced), and made an extensive trip abroad. Three years later he took part in an expedition organized by the Russian Academy of Sciences to study the East African tribes. His interest in distant lands is reflected in his verse, the first volume of which appeared in 1905. In 1912 he founded the group of acmeist poets. He fought in the First World War as a volunteer and was back in Leningrad in 1918, writing poems, translating, editing, lecturing. He had always been a monarchist and a loyal son of the Orthodox Church. In August, 1921, he was arrested and shot for participation in an anti-Soviet conspiracy. In addition to a dozen little books of original verse, he left behind various translations, including a rendering of *The Rime of the Ancient Mariner.*

Viktor Viktorovich Hofman, 1884–1911, has to his credit some short stories and two books of intimate lyrics, the second of which appeared the year before his suicide in Paris.

Vyacheslav Ivanovich Ivanov, born in 1866, embraced the profession of literature after a long and arduous preparation. The son of an official in the Surveying Department, he attended the universities of Moscow and Berlin, supplementing his academic studies with travel and years of residence in Italy. He wrote a thesis in Latin on Roman tax-farming, but his researches were devoted mainly to the cult of Dionysos. The first part of his monograph on that subject appeared in 1904, the third and last was printed nearly twenty years later in Soviet Baku. He was interested in modern thought as well, counting among his mentors Nietzsche and Dostoevsky. In 1903 he published his first book of verse. Two years later he settled in Leningrad, where his Wednesdays in the "Tower," as his apartment was known, were symposiums on poetics and religion. Several further volumes of hieratic verse and his abstruse essays confirmed his position as the pontiff of symbolism, which he kept to the end of the old regime.

When the Revolution came, it did not at once estrange him from his country. In 1921 he accepted the post of professor of Greek at the University of Azerbaijan in Baku, and for a time acted as Vice-Commissar of Education in that Soviet Republic. In 1924 he expatriated himself, settling in Italy, where he forsook the Orthodox for the Catholic Church. Shortly before the war he brought out under a Paris imprint a long, rather vacuous poem and a group of *Roman sonnets*.

Vasily Vasilyevich Kazin, born in 1898 into a workingman's family, was an alumnus of the literary studio of the Moscow Proletkult and a charter member of an association of proletarian writers founded in 1920. As a poet he was active chiefly during the early years of the Soviet era. More recently he has occupied himself with editorial work.

Velemir (Viktor Vladimirovich) Khlebnikov, 1885–1922, was born into a cultivated and fairly well-to-do family. In his middle twenties he lost interest in his university studies and took up writing. His first characteristic poems appeared in the earliest miscellanies of the futurists, and he was soon a foremost figure in their thin ranks. An avid experimenter with words, he affected a daringly neologistic style, at once infantile and pedantic, and on occasion employed "the trans-mental tongue." He was also given to elaborating rather absurd theories about language and history. Shortly after the Revolution, which like his fellow futurists he greeted with enthusiasm, he conceived a plan of setting up a world government with himself as "president of the globe," at the same time voicing disgust with all government. Later he vainly tried his hand at Soviet propaganda. Leading the life of a half-starved vagrant, he yet managed to produce a mass of verse and prose, which belongs to the world's most bizarre literature. It has been collected in five volumes, which were published in 1928–33. Mayakovsky called him "the Columbus of new poetic continents" and acknowledged him as one of his masters.

Vladislav Felitzianovich Khodasevich, 1886–1939, who is usually grouped with the symbolists, published his first book of poems in 1908.

He also managed to bring out two volumes of verse in the early years of the Soviet regime, during which he suffered severe hardships. In 1922 he expatriated himself. The émigré wrote criticism and engaged in journalism. His last book, published in Brussels the year of his death, is a volume of literary reminiscences.

Semyon Osipovich Kirsanov, born in 1906 of poor parents—his father was a tailor—received a university education and broke into print at the age of twenty. A disciple of Mayakovsky, he has composed lyrics as well as long narrative poems, notably *The Five-Year Plan* (1931). This the *Soviet Literary Encyclopedia* accords qualified praise, stating that the author has failed to grasp "the dialectic meaning of socialist construction." In 1947 he published a poetic drama entitled *Heaven Over My Country.*

Nikolay Alexeyevich Kluyev, 1887–1937, was born in a remote northern village. At an early age he started composing poems, the substance of which derived from the routine of rural life and the symbolism of the mystic sect to which his family belonged. He began by hymning the Revolution, expecting it to bring forth a peasant paradise, but in the twenties he turned against the new order. As a result, his writings were stigmatized as "the pronouncement of a *kulak* gone berserk" and he was eventually deported to Siberia. In prison and exile he continued writing verse, but his manuscripts of course remained unpublished and seem to have been lost.

Alexey Vasilyevich Koltzov, 1809–1842, was the son of a fairly prosperous cattle dealer from the steppe region who was still much of a peasant. He received an extremely scanty schooling, his father having taken him into the business at an early age. The youth, unhappy in the sordid atmosphere of his home in Voronezh, during his few leisure hours turned to reading books and writing verse in the style of folksongs. On a business trip to Moscow he ran into several literati, who took an interest in him and encouraged him to write. His new friends brought out a little book of his poems, the only one to appear in his lifetime, in 1835. Thereafter Koltzov made other trips to the two capitals, where he met the eminent literary figures of the day, including Pushkin, and, like another Burns, dinnered wi' lairds. After he returned from a stay in Moscow or Petersburg, he felt even more wretched at home, where his literary ambitions were jeered at. Moreover, his intercourse with the intellectuals led him to lamentable attempts at philosophical poetry. His life, embittered by the increased hostility of his family and wrecked by a disastrous connection with a courtesan, came to an untimely end.

Not many years after his death, Koltzov attained the status of a minor classic, his poems finding their way into school readers and anthologies. Of the 150 pieces he wrote, nearly two-thirds have been set to music.

Mikhail Alexeyevich Kuzmin, 1875–1935?, counted a French émigré among his ancestors. He studied at the Leningrad Conservatory under Rimsky-Korsakov, and until the age of thirty confined himself to writing librettos for his own operettas. In 1905 he contributed a group of sonnets to a review and in the next two decades brought out a dozen books of poems, mostly fragile, stylized verse. The Revolution did not affect his work. While he remained in the Soviet Union, he was not of it. Exactly when and under what circumstances he died is uncertain.

Boris Lebedev is the author of a slim book of verse, dated 1940. It contains, among other pieces, a version of a Robin Hood ballad.

Mikhail Yuryevich Lermontov, 1814–1841, was descended from George Learmont, a Scottish mercenary in the Polish service, who, taken prisoner by the Russians in 1613, settled in Muscovy. The Scotsman's grandsons traced their lineage to the Learmont who fought with Malcolm against Macbeth. The poet would have been even more proudly aware of his Scottish origins, had he known that the same surname was borne by Thomas the Rhymer, the thirteenth century bard who is said to have received his poetic and prophetic gifts from the Fairy Queen.

His mother, who had been deserted by her husband, died when the boy, the sole offspring of the unhappy marriage, was two years old, and he became a bone of contention between his father, a country squire in moderate circumstances, and his wealthy, highborn, and overbearing maternal grandmother. It was she who brought him up and did everything to spoil him. His early education was of the usual imported variety, and it was not until, at the age of fourteen, he entered the Boarding School for Nobles attached to the University of Moscow that he became acquainted with Russian poetry. He was extraordinarily precocious in love as in literature. Between the ages of fourteen and eighteen he wrote three hundred lyrics, fifteen long narrative poems, three dramas, and one prose tale. He first fell in love at eleven and, in spite of an unprepossessing exterior, excelled in breaking hearts.

At twenty he graduated from a military school and received his commission, having previously attended the University of Moscow. Thereafter the young hussar plunged into a giddy existence, one element of which was what he had earlier called "poetry drowned in champagne." His verse began to appear in the magazines, but it was his angry elegy on Pushkin's death, which circulated in manuscript, that brought him fame, and also transfer to a regiment stationed in the Caucasus, by way of punishment for a piece of writing judged subversive. Indeed, his mind was hospitable to ideas of political liberty.

He stayed less than a year in the Caucasus, but in 1840 was again "banished" there for having fought a duel. That romantic land deeply impressed itself on his imagination. It is the locale of his remarkable *A*

Hero of Our Time, a work of prose, as well as of his major poems, *The Novice* and *The Demon*. A few months after his second departure for the Caucasus, a collection of his poems appeared between covers, the only book of his verse to be issued during his lifetime. Much of his work, including *The Demon*, was published posthumously.

When not in exile, Lermontov lived in the capital, moving in the beau monde, which he both sought after and despised, and generally eschewing literary circles. Morbidly sensitive and hungry for affection, he chose to hide his real self under a frivolous and arrogant exterior. During his last sojourn in the Caucasus, he saw action in the fighting against the natives. Spared by their bullets, the young poet was killed in a duel with a fellow officer who had been the butt of his merciless gibes.

Nikolay Lvov is a newcomer on the literary scene.

Apollon Nikolayevich Maikov, 1821–1897, was brought up by a mother with literary leanings and an aristocratic father who gave up a military career for that of a painter. He himself studied painting, but early turned to literature, publishing his first volume of verse in 1842. The book brought him instant renown and a government stipend, and was followed at rather long intervals by other collections of poems. Much of his work has to do with antiquity—he had enjoyed a thorough classical education—some of his best known pieces being in the manner of the Greek anthology. He also wrote Russian idyls, patriotic lyrics, and poems on historical subjects. The conflict of early Christianity with imperial Rome is the theme of three of his long dramatic poems, including his major work, *Two Worlds* (1881). An epicurean and an aesthete, Maikov was, not surprisingly, a man of conservative views. For nearly half a century he faithfully served his monarch as a censor.

Osip Emilyevich Mandelstamm, 1891–1942?, in his middle teens was active in the Party of Socialist-Revolutionaries. Before long, however, he lost his taste for politics and turned to poetry, becoming an admirer of Baudelaire and Verlaine. Yet his own poems were not in the symbolist manner. A slim collection of his verse appeared in 1913, and almost ten years later he brought out two more collections of poems. He is also the author of some autobiographic sketches and of "a lyrical tale" in prose.

According to the *Soviet Literary Encyclopedia*, before 1925 his work was marked by "absolute social indifferentism," and his later work betrayed hostility toward the new order. A selection from his verse, published in 1928, seems to have been his last appearance in print, although he presumably went on writing. It is said that he composed an epigram on Stalin and as a result was deported, but eventually was allowed to return to Moscow. He seems to have been deported a second time, and he died under obscure circumstances.

Anatoly Borisovich Marienhof, born in 1897, started his literary career in the early years of the Revolution. He called himself an imagist and wrote verse calculated to startle and waylay. In 1928 he published a novel (available in English under the title *The Cynics*) about his friend Yesenin. More recently he has written a play or two.

Mikhail Lvovich Matusovsky, born in 1915, attended a trade school and was employed as a construction worker before he entered the Literary Institute of the Union of Soviet Writers. During the recent war he published three books of verse. His services as poet and war correspondent were rewarded with decorations and medals.

Vladimir Vladimirovich Mayakovsky, 1893–1930, the child of Great Russian parents, was born in a Transcaucasian village. He was thirteen when, upon the father's death, the family moved to Moscow, exchanging comfort for poverty. Two years later he joined the Bolshevist faction of the Socialist Party and quitted high school, rather than incur the disabilities attached to expulsion. The youthful agitator was soon arrested and served several short prison terms, and about this time he started writing verse. On his release he went to an art school, but was expelled for publications and public appearances that smacked of scandal. He signed a futurist manifesto for a miscellany printed in 1912 under the title, *A Slap in the Face of Public Taste.* He continued to flabbergast the public with sartorial extravagances and with collections of futurist verse published under such titles as *A Cloud in Pants.* Between 1913 and 1916 he brought out three such collections and a verse tragedy entitled *Vladimir Mayakovsky.*

At a public meeting which took place shortly after the October Revolution he summoned the artists to hail the Soviet power. He soon developed an enormous activity in the service of the new regime. He painted three thousand posters and composed six thousand rhymed slogans for Rosta (Russian Telegraph Agency), the Soviet publicity bureau, which employed him from 1919 to 1921. He wrote marching songs, an ode to the Revolution, and a May Day poem that he recited at open-air meetings. In numerous pieces, some of them written to order, he exhorted, explained, jeered, boasted, threatened, all in behalf of Soviet policy. The several plays from his pen were less successful than his poems. He headed the Moscow Association of Futurists and later edited two reviews speaking for "the Left Front" in the arts. Traveling all over the country, he declaimed his verse before audiences made up of soldiers, workers, students, children. He was proud of being the megaphone of Bolshevism. He also made frequent trips abroad; in 1925 he visited Mexico and spent three months in the United States, the spectacle of this seat of capitalism moving him to indignant, if unimpressive, utterance. Though he had emphatically condemned Yesenin for having committed suicide, Mayakovsky ended his own stormy career by shooting himself.

Since his death his work—in 1939–1949(?) it was collected in twelve volumes edited with the scholarly care accorded a classic—has been the object of boundless admiration.

Dmitry Sergeyevich Merezhkovsky, 1866–1941, the son of a high government official, was able to gratify his desire for study and foreign travel. On graduating from the university, he married Zinaida Hippius, the poet, who was to be his lifelong helpmate. He had himself been writing verse for some time, his first book of poems having appeared in 1888. Except for a few pieces composed in his old age, all his original verse—an accomplished Hellenist, he translated several Greek tragedies—is contained in one volume, first published in 1910. By that time he had acquired a great reputation as a literary critic, a publicist, and especially as an historical novelist. All his work was dominated by the religion of "the Third Testament," which was a synthesis of flesh and spirit, paganism and Christianity.

In 1920 Merezhkovsky and his wife left Russia, finally settling in France. Abroad he spoke out vigorously against Bolshevism, which was to him the apocalyptic Beast. With great industry he continued to turn out historical novels and fictional biographies, but these were now failures. He outlived his popularity and died in Paris (on the day of the Pearl Harbor attack), a forgotten man.

N. Minsky (Nikolay Maximovich Vilenkin), 1855–1937, the son of an impecunious Jewish villager, managed to get a good classical education and a law degree. He did not, however, practice the profession for which he had been trained. Even before he was out of school he achieved popularity with reflective lyrics in the civic and humanitarian manner of the period. His first book of verse appeared in 1887, a previous collection having been destroyed by order of the censor. Shortly thereafter he began to champion amoral individualism and aestheticism, though his own verse did not always exemplify this outlook. In a series of essays he elaborated a metaphysics of nonbeing—he called it Meonism—which is a bizarre variety of philosophical idealism. He also composed several plays and translated *The Iliad.*

The radicalism of his youth came briefly to life in 1905. In the last weeks of that eventful year he was the nominal editor of the first openly published Bolshevik newspaper, of which the actual editor was Lenin. In its columns appeared Minsky's "Workers' Hymn" which opened with the line: "Proletarians of all lands, unite!" When the manifesto of the Soviet of Workers' Deputies appeared in its twenty-seventh issue, the paper was suppressed and Minsky found himself threatened with a prison sentence. He managed to make his way to France, where he remained for the rest of his days, living as an obscure journalist. His association with the Bolsheviks had been in the nature of a passing episode. He had no sympathy with their methods, and when in 1917 they inaugurated the Soviet regime, he denounced them in the French press.

Nikolay Alexeyevich Nekrasov, 1821–January 8, 1878 (December 27, 1877, Old Style), in his early years observed the worst excesses of serfdom, since his father was a brutal, dissolute country squire who, after retiring from the army, had become a rural police officer. From his frail, gentle mother he may have derived the ideal of womanhood that he kept all his life. After attending a secondary school for a few years, at seventeen he was sent to Petersburg to enter a military school. He defied his father's will by enrolling in the university as an auditor—he had failed to pass the entrance examinations—and therewith was thrown on his own resources.

For several years he was a starving hack, yet in 1840 he managed to bring out at his own cost a little volume of verse, a deserved fiasco. Before long he made a successful entrance into the publishing field. At twenty-five the hardheaded, wide-awake young man was the co-owner and moving spirit of a monthly and, incidentally, the lover of his partner's wife. Under his guidance the magazine grew in importance and during the stormy sixties was the organ of the democratic intelligentsia. When, in 1866, it was suppressed, Nekrasov acquired another magazine. The flower of Russian prose appeared in the pages of the two periodicals, along with Nekrasov's own poems. These were first collected in a volume in 1856, and as new pieces came from his pen, the book was reissued in successive augmented editions. From the first, its success was enormous. His poems, with their libertarian and Populist message, were the Bible of the radical youth. Those that were barred by censorship were circulated in manuscript or appeared in the underground press. Some of his verse joined the body of popular balladry. Not a little of his verse is in the vein of folk poetry. As a successful author and publisher, Nekrasov lived extravagantly, in spite of ethical scruples that dictated poems of self-scorn.

He was particularly productive in the last decade of his life, when he wrote *Russian Women* and *Who Lives Happily in Russia?*, his major works, conceived on an epic scale. He completed these amidst the cruel sufferings of his last illness. To the end he continued to write verse. On his deathbed he married a woman of the people who had shared his life in his last years. At the time of his death, he was considered by many the greatest Russian poet, barring none, not even Pushkin. His posthumous reputation, after suffering an eclipse at the turn of the century, has more recently regained its luster.

Nikolay Novosyolov is a member of the rising generation of writers.

Pyotr Vasilyevich Oreshin, born in 1887, is usually classed as "a peasant poet." His collected verse, in three volumes, appeared in 1923–1927. Thereafter he wrote chiefly fiction. Since the early thirties he has not been heard from.

Sergey Orlov is a young man whose verse has been anthologized, although it has apparently been published in magazines only.

Sergey Ostrovoy is a new name on the roster of Soviet poets.

Boris Leonidovich Pasternak was born in Moscow in 1890. His mother was a gifted musician, his father a noted painter who, unlike the son, found some material for his work in his Jewish background. In his teens he prepared himself to become a composer; he was then under the spell of Scriabine, a friend of the family. Later he gave up music for philosophy, studying at the universities of Moscow and Marburg. With the outbreak of the First World War he returned to Russia and for two years was employed in an industrial plant in the Urals. After the Revolution he held for a while a minor post in the Commissariat of Education. He has since lived by his pen.

He broke into print with a book of verse, *The Twin in Clouds,* in 1914. Three years later appeared another small group of his poems entitled *Above the Barriers.* The early years of the Soviet era were those of his greatest productivity. In addition to short lyrics, he published several long poems, one of them dealing with an episode in the Revolution of 1905. His total output is as slight as it is distinguished: his verse was collected in one moderately sized volume in 1933. He has since published little original verse, a score or so of his poems having appeared during the recent war. He has been devoting himself chiefly to translation, turning into Russian some of Shelley's and Keats's lyrics and several of Shakespeare's plays, among other things. He has also written an autobiographical fragment, dedicated to the memory of Rainer Maria Rilke, and several stories couched in a most unconventional prose.

In spite of the esoteric quality of his work, Pasternak has a considerable following at home. In 1934 he was elected to the Board of the Union of Soviet Writers. Officialdom, however, views his verse with suspicion, and the critics have been scathing in condemning it for its nonpolitical character.

Karolina Karlovna Pavlova, née Janisch, 1807–1893, was the daughter of a German professor settled in Moscow. Her family having prevented her from becoming the wife of Adam Mickiewicz, the great Polish poet, she married a minor Russian novelist. During the last three decades of her life she lived in Germany.

The first Russian woman of letters to achieve any prominence, she began by translating Russian verse into French and German, but in the forties and fifties she contributed to the magazines a considerable number of original poems in Russian. A collection of these was published separately in 1863, the only book of hers to appear during her lifetime. She wrote chiefly personal lyrics, though some of her poems carried the message of Slavophilism. In her own day her work was dismissed as "butterfly verse," but her careful craftsmanship—poetry was to her "a sacred métier"—endeared her to the modernists.

Nikolay Gavrilovich Poletayev, 1889–1935, a child of city slums, blossomed out as an author only after the Revolution. He attended the literary studio of the Moscow Proletkult and was a member of the Moscow group of proletarian poets that called itself The Forge. Between 1918 and 1932 he published a collection of stories about railway workers—he was himself a railway clerk—and half a dozen thin volumes of verse.

Yakov Petrovich Polonsky, 1820–1898, the son of a civil servant, was a prolific, if undistinguished, novelist and did much editorial work. Although a censor for many years, he was a man of moderately liberal views. In his old age, however, he became conservative and turned to religion. Between 1844, when he published his first book of poems, and 1890, when his last volume appeared, he produced a great deal of miscellaneous verse. His lyrics were at one time very popular, and many of them were set to music.

Alexander Sergeyevich Pushkin, 1799–1837, descended on his father's side from an old, patrician, though by no means opulent, family; his maternal great-grandfather was a Negro, or, according to one account, "an African Moor from Abyssinia." The poet liked to allude to his exotic origins and made his black ancestor the hero of his first novel.

Instructed as a child by French tutors, he graduated at the age of eighteen from a boarding school for the scions of the nobility, an indifferent scholar, but already looked upon in *avant-garde* circles as a poet of the highest promise. For three years he remained in Petersburg (Leningrad), holding a clerkship at the Ministry of Foreign Affairs, but chiefly engaged in versifying and in sowing wild oats. Because he composed some poems in praise of liberty and a few barbed epigrams against highly stationed personages, he found himself, in the spring of 1820, transferred to a remote southern section of the empire. Several months later his first book, a fairy tale in verse, appeared in the capital.

The banished poet spent two years in Bessarabia, traveled in the Crimea and the Caucasus and made a stay at Odessa. During those years he wrote not only lyrics but also long narrative poems, which established his reputation as "the Byron of Russia." He also started his major work, *Eugene Onegin,* a novel in verse, which was not printed in full until 1833.

"Exile" did not have the sobering effect on Pushkin that the authorities had counted on and, as a result, in the summer of 1824 he was dismissed from the service and confined to his family estate. There he composed many short lyrics, some derived from such diverse sources as Russian folklore and the Koran; he also wrote an historical play in blank verse, *Boris Godunov*. In September, 1826, his banishment finally came to an end. In fact, he became a protégé of the czar, the latter undertaking to censor his writings in person. The situation had its drawbacks, and in any event the poet remained a political suspect, kept under police surveillance and forbidden to travel abroad.

Back in the capital, Pushkin resumed the giddy, undisciplined life to which he was accustomed, but managed to turn out much verse, including a long poem about Peter the Great and Mazeppa, and he also composed several dramatic sketches and a group of short stories. At the age of thirty-one he married a society girl who, he said, was his 113th love. She was beautiful, but empty-headed and coldhearted. Although his frivolous young wife's social ambitions interfered with his work, he was now writing some of his finest lyrics and his best prose. He also produced a work of history and started editing a review.

In his last years Pushkin was beset by many harassments. His income was insufficient to meet the needs of his growing family and, in spite of a subvention from the czar, his debts kept mounting. A court appointment, which he had accepted for his wife's sake, was another source of vexation. And then he suspected her of infidelity. In an access of jealousy, he provoked an admirer of hers, who had recently become her brother-in-law, to offer him a challenge. In the duel the poet was fatally wounded.

Nikolay Rylenkov's verse first appeared in print during the recent war. In 1943–1944 he brought out three slender books of poems.

Kondraty Fyodorovich Ryleyev, 1795–1826, like not a few of his fellow officers, was infected with liberalism while campaigning against Napoleon in western Europe. Retiring from the army in his early twenties, he settled in the capital, married, and took a post, first in the judiciary and then in the administration of the Russian-American Company, which traded in Alaska. In 1823 he joined a secret society pledged to bring about the downfall of the autocracy and the establishment of representative government in Russia. For some time he had been contributing poems to reviews and miscellanies, and in 1825 he published two slim books: a long poem and a collection of historical ballads. They carried a protest against despotism, as did his imitations of folksongs. In the days that followed the death of Alexander I, he took a leading part in organizing the military insurrection of December 14 (26), 1825. When this proved a miserable fiasco, he was seized and, with four other Decembrists, hanged. Some of his poems were circulated in manuscript and in clandestine editions.

E. Serebrovskaya has only recently broken into print, and no information about her is available.

Igor Vasilyevich Severyanin (Lotaryov), born in 1887, began his literary career in 1913 with the publication of a book of poems. At that time he was closely identified with a tiny group of versifiers who styled themselves egofuturists. With fatal facility he went on writing quantities of vacuous, occasionally melodious verse. When the Revolution came, he expatriated himself. Seventeen volumes of his collected verse appeared between 1916 and 1922, the early part of the edition in Moscow, the later in Dorpat (Tartu) and Berlin. He seems to have made his last appearance in print with a book of sonnets published in Belgrade in 1934.

Stepan Petrovich Shchipachev, born in 1899 into a peasant family, joined the Communist Party at the age of twenty and entered the Red Army. During the civil war copies of his poems—he had been writing verse for some time—were dropped from a plane into the trenches of the Whites. Since 1931 he has published more than a score of slight books of verse. In the recent war he worked on a trench newspaper, and received several decorations and medals.

Zinaida Shishova wrote a few youthful lyrics, which were printed in the early years of the Revolution. Then she disappeared from literature until 1943 when she published a novel about the Wat Tyler rebellion and a remarkable long poem on the blockade of Leningrad.

Konstantin Mikhailovich Simonov, born in 1915, worked as a mechanic before enrolling in the Literary Institute of the Union of Soviet Writers, from which he graduated in 1938. That year he brought out his first collection of poems. He achieved great popularity during the recent war with his patriotic lyrics, his war dispatches in the Red Army newspaper, his plays, and his Stalingrad novel, *Days and Nights,* which received the Stalin prize. In 1946 he toured the United States, and subsequently wrote an uncomplimentary play about life in America, which was a great success at home.

Fyodor Kuzmich Sologub (Teternikov), 1863–1927, was the son of a tailor and grew up in a house where his widowed mother was a servant. For ten years after his graduation at the age of nineteen from a normal school, he taught in the provinces, learning to know the Main Streets of Russia, which were to furnish the stuff of his fiction. In 1892 he removed to the capital, where his uncanny verse and short stories soon gave him entrée to the circle of modernist poets, his first book of poems appearing four years later. Thus, unlike the other symbolists, he came to literature as a mature man. He continued to teach until 1907, meanwhile producing much verse and prose, as well as some closet plays, so that his collected works, brought out just before the outbreak of the First World War, comprised twenty volumes, of which five contained verse.

After the Revolution he continued to write without attempting to adjust himself to the new conditions, and several of his books appeared under Russian imprints, as well as in Sofia, Tallinn, Berlin. In 1922 he brought out a little collection of frivolous *bergerettes*—a gesture of aloofness so complete as to be audacious. His sixtieth birthday was the occasion of a public celebration by the thin ranks of the old guard, but it was now practically impossible for him to publish his writings. He had always been a stay-at-home, but so completely was he out of sympathy with Bolshevism that he was eager to leave the country. When the necessary papers had at last been obtained, his wife committed suicide, and he became too apathetic to make use of them. He was thus spared death in exile.

His work has been neglected in Soviet Russia, only one volume of selections from his poems having been issued posthumously (in 1939) and only one of his novels having been reprinted.

Vladimir Sergeyevich Solovyov, 1853–1900, the grandson of a priest and the son of an eminent historian, was himself a systematic thinker, but also a mystic and a visionary, whose asceticism was the obverse of his powerfully erotic nature. After receiving his degree from the University of Moscow, he traveled abroad and on his return became a university instructor, but his academic career ended abruptly when shortly after the assassination of Alexander II he delivered a public lecture in which he urged the new czar to forbear punishing his father's assassins in a spirit of Christian forgiveness. Thenceforth he devoted himself to elaborating, in a series of imposing treatises, a theological doctrine which is Russia's main contribution to religious philosophy. He also wrote a good deal on literature and public affairs. One of his cardinal concepts was the Eternal Feminine, which he identified with Sophia: Divine Wisdom. He claimed to have beheld her with his own eyes on three occasions. He first glimpsed her in Moscow when he was nine. He next saw her, thirteen years later, in the reading room of the British Museum, as he pored over abstruse mystical writings. She bade him to follow her to Egypt. Arriving in Cairo, he went afoot into the desert and there beheld his beatific vision for the last time. These experiences are the subject of a poem which he composed, after another trip to Egypt, two years before his death. From time to time in the last twenty-five years of his short life, he produced lyrics marked by spirituality and high seriousness, as well as verse in a comic vein. His poems, first printed in magazines, in 1891 were collected in a volume, two enlarged editions of which were published within Solovyov's lifetime, some of his lyrics appearing only posthumously.

Lubov Nikitishna Stolitza, née Yershova, was born in 1884. Though the daughter of a coachman, she received a good education. Between 1908 and 1916 she brought out three books of poems, a novel in verse, and several playlets. In 1918 she expatriated herself and disappeared from the literary scene.

Alexey Alexandrovich Surkov, born in 1899 into a peasant family, went to work at an early age, served in the Red Army, held various posts in the Communist Party as organizer and journalist, and at the age of thirty-five graduated from the Institute of Red Professors. In the decade preceding the Second World War he published several collections of verse. Many of his lyrics, for instance, "The Song About Stalin," were set to music and gained considerable currency. More recently he has achieved even greater popularity. The verse he has turned out since 1941 forms a kind of rhymed chronicle of the war. He has received several marks of official recognition, including the Stalin prize for literature.

Ludmila Tatyanicheva belongs to the youngest generation of Russian verse writers.

Nikolay Semyonovich Tikhonov, born in 1896, came from a poor home and did not receive much of an education, attending a commercial high school. He fought in the first World War and helped to defend Leningrad from the Whites. Spirited and fond of adventure, he traveled in the outlying parts of the Union, and tried several occupations, acting among them, before he turned to literature, which to him then meant poetry. His first collection of poems appeared in 1922. Other books of verse, as well as of prose, followed, though his output has been rather small, even if his translations, chiefly of Georgian poetry, are included. In his youth he belonged to the Serapion Brothers, a confraternity of writers who in the midst of revolution were bold enough to champion political neutrality, and he confessed publicly to a weakness for anarchism. Eventually he underwent a change of heart and became a leading exponent of Communist literary policy. Indeed, from 1944 until the purge in the field of the arts which took place in the summer of 1946, he held the important post of chairman of the board of the Union of Soviet Writers. During the recent war he wrote a series of stories in which he celebrated the heroism of Leningrad, and also composed some verse, including a patriotic poem which won him the Stalin prize.

Count Alexey Konstantinovich Tolstoy, 1817–1875, came of the same old aristocratic line that was to give the world Leo Tolstoy. He sat on Goethe's knees and was a playmate of Emperor Alexander II. A fairly good education enhanced by foreign travel, a great fortune and the highest court connections held out the promise of a brilliant bureaucratic career, but he was jealous of his independence and preferred to be an artist. Among his friends he counted Gogol, Nekrasov, Turgenev, and in his late thirties he broke into print with a group of poems. In the score of years that he filled with literary activity, he produced a considerable amount of verse, in addition to an historical novel and a trilogy of plays testifying to his dramatic talent and an ability to evoke his country's past. The volume of his poems which came out in 1867 was the only one to appear during his lifetime, not a little of his work having been collected only posthumously. In addition to long narrative pieces, he wrote ballads in the folk manner and satires poking fun at both the radicals and official-dom.

An aristocrat by conviction as well as by birth, he abhorred the materialism of his time and regarded the doctrine of equality as "the foolish invention of 1793," but he also despised the parasitic bureaucrats ruling in the name of an irresponsible autocrat. There was a strong comic streak in his make-up: with the aid of two other writers he perpetrated an elaborate hoax on the public, inventing an author by the name of Kozma Prutkov and providing him with a biography and works. These consisted of aphorisms, skits, parodies, and other facetiae. Tolstoy's reputation as a poet rests chiefly on his lyrics and ballads. Many of them have been set to music by eminent Russian composers.

Alexander Trifonovich Tvardovsky, born in 1910, the son of a village blacksmith, received scanty schooling. Until the age of eighteen he stayed at home, doing chores and helping in the smithy. Then he tried his hand at journalism in Smolensk, and in 1930 published a long poem, *The Road to Socialism,* on collective farming, the problem of the moment. Another long poem on the same subject, published six years later, made his name widely known and won him the Stalin prize for literature. He also wrote a good deal of prose aiming to promote rural collectivization. At the same time he was closing the gaps in his education, graduating from the University of Moscow in 1939, just a year after he joined the Communist Party. During the war he achieved immense popularity with a long narrative poem about "Vasily Tyorkin," the Soviet equivalent of G.I. Joe. In 1946 he completed another verse cycle dealing with postwar reconstruction.

Fyodor Ivanovich Tyutchev, 1803–1873, came of an old line of noblemen said to have been founded by a Venetian who, after accompanying Marco Polo on his travels, had settled in Russia. A member of a precocious generation, he graduated from the University of Moscow at eighteen and was shortly thereafter appointed to the staff of the Russian embassy at Munich. For over a score of years he remained abroad, where he married in succession two aristocratic Bavarian widows, to whom he was devoted if not faithful. On returning to Russia, he continued in the diplomatic service, but did not advance far, partly because of an open extramarital union of long duration, which he erroneously called his last love. During the final two decades of his life he held the post of censor, not inappropriate to a man of conservative convictions. In 1848, when thrones were shaking all over Europe, he wrote an essay in which he predicted that Orthodox Russia, at the head of the United Slavs, would be the sacred ark riding the waves of the Western revolutionary deluge.

Tyutchev had not been long abroad when poems from his pen began to appear in the miscellanies and magazines. During the forties his name practically vanished from the public prints, but the revolutionary upheaval with which the decade closed in western Europe moved him to write a series of political poems. In 1850 his verse was enthusiastically commented upon in the leading monthly, but it was four years later, when about a hundred of his lyrics were issued separately, owing to the efforts of his friend Turgenev, that he achieved a standing with the general public. Only one other more complete collection of his verse appeared during the poet's lifetime (in 1868). After his death his reputation, based on a slight but distinguished body of work, continued to grow steadily, particularly after the turn of the century, when the symbolists rediscovered him and hailed him as a great forerunner.

Marina Ivanovna Tzvetayeva, 1892–1942, was schooled in her native city of Moscow and abroad. Between 1910 and 1922, when she expatriated herself, she published eight little books of verse. She also has several plays and stories to her credit. Abroad she continued to write, taking a sharp anti-Soviet stand, but shortly before the war she returned to Russia. Not long thereafter she hanged herself.

Dmitry Vladimirovich Venevitinov, 1805–1827, was of gentle birth. He received a good education and was a student of the Romantic German philosophy of his time. Like Pushkin, to whom he was related, he sympathized with the aims of the Decembrists, but did not participate in their conspiracy against the autocracy. He left behind some forty original poems and a few translations and essays, dying before he could fulfill his brilliant promise. His work was published between covers only posthumously.

Maximilian Alexandrovich Voloshin, 1877–1932, a native of Kiev, was of mixed Cossack and German stock. His earliest impressions were associated with the Crimea, and at Koktebel, on the eastern littoral of that Hellenic promontory of the Scythian plain, he eventually found a home to which he became passionately attached. He was expelled from the University of Moscow for participation in student disorders and deported to Tashkent. On being released from exile, he traveled in Italy and Greece, discovering in the Mediterranean what he was to call "the fatherland of my spirit." Then came Paris and French poetry, which, he said, taught him rhythm and form. In his middle twenties he took up painting, and at the same time began to contribute verse to *avant-garde* periodicals, but the first collection of his poems did not come out until 1910. Another volume of his lyrics appeared at the height of World War I, but contained no war poems.

The Revolution put an end to his complete aloofness from the contemporary scene. A note of mystic patriotism came into his lyrics and he wrote poems about the Red Terror which no Soviet censor could have passed and which appeared abroad. He did not expatriate himself, yet remained remarkably free from official molestation. In his last decade he published nothing. Clad in the classical Greek garb he affected, he led the life of a hermit in his beloved Koktebel and became a legend long before he died there, an exile in his own country, if ever there was one.

Prince Pyotr Andreyevich Vyazemsky, 1792–1871, scion of an old family and sole heir to a great fortune, eventually discarded the liberal opinions of his youth and made a brilliant bureaucratic career. As a poet, he was a dilettante who wrote chiefly light satirical pieces in the manner of the French classicists, but he was a serious and penetrating literary critic. In his prime a member of the aristocratic group then dominating Russian literature, he was an enemy of the democratic trend which set in during his latter years.

Sergey Alexandrovich Yesenin, 1895–1925, was brought up by his grandparents, fairly well-to-do peasants who were devout Old Believers. At the age of seventeen he left his native village in the province of Ryazan for Moscow. There he attended courses in a people's university. Two years later, already a budding poet, he found himself in Leningrad, where his first book of verse appeared in 1916. That year he was drafted into the army, but deserted when the Revolution broke out. He greeted it with enthusiasm. Following the Soviet government to Moscow, he became a familiar figure in the literary cafés there, breaking away occasionally to go off on trips to outlying sections of the country. His brief, tempestuous marriage to Isadora Duncan (1922–1923) gave him a chance to make the grand tour, which included the United States. He had long had a weakness for drink, but now he was rarely sober. His loss of faith in the Revolution may have contributed to his growing rowdyism and bohemian bravado. When, in 1923, he returned to Russia, he did a good deal of writing, but his work clearly showed the mental deterioration due to drink and cocaine. Under the influence of alcohol he was given to fits of violence which necessitated the intervention of the police. In the winter of 1925, after some weeks in a psychiatric institution, he hanged himself with a strap from his suitcase. The previous day he had complained to a friend that he could find no ink in the wretched hotel where he was stopping and handed him a poem written in his own blood.

For so short and disordered a life, Yesenin's output was not inconsiderable. In addition to lyrics, he composed several long poems and a drama in verse. His one prose tale is without merit.

Mikhail Alexandrovich Zenkevich, born in 1888 into a schoolteacher's family, studied law at the University of Petersburg and philosophy in Vienna and Berlin. He published his first book of verse in 1912. Two others followed in 1918 and 1926. He seems to have adjusted himself to Soviet conditions without submerging his distinctive style, but in the last fifteen years he has been rather inactive, except as editor and translator. In 1947 he brought out an anthology of American poetry.

Vasily Andreyevich Zhukovsky, 1783–1852, was the illegitimate son of an aged country squire and a Turkish woman taken captive by one of his serfs and presented to him as a war trophy. Adopted by his godfather, the boy attended a school for the nobility, and afterward continued to enlarge his knowledge of history and especially of the Western languages and literatures. When Napoleon invaded Russia, he joined the army as a volunteer, but soon retired from the service. He was then already famous as the author of sentimental ballads and patriotic poems and as a translator of German and English verse. For nearly a quarter of a century he was a tutor to royalty, and he took advantage of his high connections to intercede in behalf of erring men of letters, such as Pushkin, and to alleviate the lot of political prisoners. He continued to turn out many translations and adaptations, and a little original verse. At the age of fifty-eight he married a German girl of eighteen and went to live in Germany. In his last years he produced, among other translations, an admirable version of the entire *Odyssey* and of a part of *The Iliad.*

Index of Authors Represented

Index of Titles

312